ACH
①
2768

Th
star
ano
stan

CL.16

25

25..

26 MAR. 198

14 MAY 198

1 200252 001 97

ANNO DOMINI 1568
ET ANNO ÆTATIS SVÆ

ENGLISH PISTOLS

Howard L. Blackmore

THE ARMOURIES
H.M. TOWER OF LONDON

ARMS AND ARMOUR
PRESS

Published in 1985
by The Trustees of the Armouries,
H.M. Tower of London, London EC3N 4AB.

with Arms and Armour Press
2–6 Hampstead High Street, London NW3 1QQ

Produced for The Armouries by
Arms and Armour Press

British Library Cataloguing in Publication Data:
Blackmore, Howard L.
English pistols.
1. Pistols, English – History
I. Title
683.4'3'0942   TS537
ISBN 0-948092-00-9 (Armouries)
ISBN 0-85368-712-9 (A&AP)

Printed in Italy in association with
Keats European Limited
by Tipolitografia G. Canale & C. S.p.A. - Turin

Introduction

The first illustrations of guns in Europe appear in English manuscripts of 1326/7, and the first 'hand gonnes' are mentioned in the 1380s. Judging by existing specimens, the barrels were often as short as a 'span' or nine inches in length; but they had to be mounted on wooden poles or crude stocks. Two hands were then necessary to use them; one to hold the gun, the other to ignite the touch-hole with a hand-held match. The essential quality of a pistol is that it can be held and fired with one hand. No real pistols could be designed, therefore, until some form of mechanical ignition or gun lock had been invented.

The first gun lock was probably the matchlock, introduced in the 15th century, in which the smouldering match was held in the jaws of a curved metal arm or serpentine, and brought down into the priming pan by the action of a lever or trigger. But it was unsuitable for pistols and, apart from isolated examples (and toy pistols), the only extensive application of the matchlock to pistol-length barrels was in the pistol-shields made for Henry VIII's bodyguard. Henry VIII, very much a man-at-arms, amassed a great armoury, which, according to an inventory prepared in 1547, included a number of pistols then known as 'dags' or 'tackes'. Some were colourfully decorated, the metal parts gilded and the stocks covered with velvet or bone. They were also described as being armed with 'fier lockes' or wheellocks.

In the wheellock the vital sparks to ignite the priming powder next to the touch-hole were produced by a serrated wheel rotating rapidly against a piece of iron pyrites. Once the wheellock of a pistol was 'spanned' or wound up by a key, it could be carried and fired at will simply by squeezing the trigger. This self-igniting weapon became a much-prized personal arm. Portraits of Elizabethan gentlemen such as those of Sir Martin Frobisher, painted in 1577, and Sir William Drury, 1575, show them proudly holding wheellock pistols. Some of these Elizabethan paintings depict their subjects with pistols fitted with another form of gun lock, the snaphance or snapwork. This was an early form of flintlock, obtaining its fire from a flint, held in the jaws of a cock, striking against a steel plate swivelling over the priming pan. The word comes probably from the Dutch *Snaphaan*, a pecking cock.

The flintlock became an English speciality, and the Venetian author of *Instruttione di Bombardieri*, in 1592, wrote with approval of the great ingenuity of the English and their guns 'which were ignited very quickly by means of a steel and a stone'. Unfortunately the new pistols could get into wrong hands, and the ageing Elizabeth I indignantly passed a proclamation in 1594 against the carrying of 'Dags otherwise called Pistols, to the terrour of all people professing to travel and live peaceably'. Such legal prohibitions were largely ignored, however, and in the same year Sir Thomas Lee had his portrait painted with a snaphance pistol. The possibility of a pistol being 'carried covertly' by an assassin was what really worried the authorities, and James I issued another proclamation in 1613 against 'pocket Dagges' or 'like Short Gunnes by what name soeuer they be, or may be called or knowen'. For some time this did restrict the manufacture of pistols to large holster pistols and the like.

By the end of the 16th century a thriving gunmaking industry had been established in East Smithfield and the Minories next to the Tower of London, whence came official orders for military arms. There were barrel-smiths, lock-makers, stock-carvers and artists responsible for a gun's decoration – damasceners or gilders of metals and inlayers of bone, ivory and mother-of-pearl. Unfortunately these craftsmen were not yet organised into a proper craft union or City Company of their own. No identifiable marks or names seem to have been used on barrels and locks, with the result that it is now difficult to recognise English pistols of this period.

But, in 1638, a Gunmakers Company was granted a Royal Charter to control manufacture, and authorised proofmarks and makers' marks began to be stamped on guns. At first the English Civil War of 1642–51 and its puritan aftermath gave little encouragement to English gunmakers to produce other than plain wheellock and flintlock pistols. Some of these were surprisingly effective. Barrels which were unscrewed for loading and could be rifled were made accurate enough for marksmen like Prince Rupert to perform, in 1642, his famous feat of hitting the weathercock on St. Mary's Church, Stafford, with his pistol at a distance of 60 paces.

The Restoration in 1660 heralded a refreshing change in pistol design. The wheellock, never popular in England, was discarded, and, with the flintlock mechanism much simplified and improved, gunmakers were able to experiment with all manner of breechloaders and repeating pistols. The Marquis of Worcester, in 1663, published his *Century of Inventions*, which included such novelties as a key pistol, a superimposed-charge pistol and a tinder-pistol. There was no obvious restriction on size, and, above all, the finely-decorated pistol was regarded as suitable for presents among princes. In 1665, Charles II presented the Czar of Russia with his own pair of pistols. After the Revocation of the Edict of Nantes in France in 1685, French and Dutch refugees like Pierre Monlong and Andrew Dolep, came to London and brought an artistry not seen on guns before. Monlong created for William III probably the most elaborately-decorated pair of pistols ever made in this country. Dolep, for his part, was instrumental in establishing the graceful form and restrained decoration which became the hallmark of the English pistol.

Throughout the reigns of Queen Anne and the first two Georges, there was a general tendency to shorten the barrels of pistols, and for some time the length of military and naval pistol barrels was standardised at 12 inches. The furniture or mounts of a pistol, i.e. the trigger-guard, side-plate, butt-cap and escutcheon-plate, were cast in plain brass for military use; in more elaborate design for civilian models; and, for the best quality, in chased and engraved silver. There was little carving or inlay on the walnut stocks of the long holster pistols; pocket and belt pistols, however, were of more fashionable appearance, the stocks often inlaid with silver wire. For these pistols also, the 17th-century form of cannon-barrel, which could be unscrewed at the breech for loading, was retained. Although made extensively during the period 1720–60, this distinctive type of pistol is today often called a 'Queen Anne' pistol. The side-plates are embellished with military trophies, but the butt-caps are nearly always in the form of grotesque masks. When made of silver, these mounts often bear London or Birmingham hallmarks, so that it is possible to date them.

While the foremost English gunmakers were always capable of creating pieces which were as much works of art as firearms, only a few like Henry Hadley and William Bailes made a point of producing pistols of outstanding decorative quality. The majority of gunmakers, or rather their customers, were more concerned with the shooting powers of their pistols. The blued or bright barrels of Spanish makers and the browned, twisted Damascus barrels of Persia and Turkey were admired for their strength and appearance, and were often fitted to English pistols. This concern for accuracy came to a head in about 1770 with the introduction of the duelling pistol. With long, light barrels, they were carefully sighted and the ·locks were furnished with adjustable hair-triggers that could be set to the nerves of the shooter. Pistols which had been previously sold in thick, brightly-coloured woollen bags were now supplied in oak or mahogany cases complete with all the accessories necessary for careful loading and maintenance. A cased pair of pistols was now *de rigueur* for all travelling gentlemen and officers.

The late Georgian period was the hey-day of the flintlock pistol made by such gifted craftsmen as John Twigg, John and Joseph Manton, Durs and Joseph Egg, Henry Nock and Ezekiel Baker. These men were encouraged by the patronage of George IV and the fanaticism of sportsmen-writers like Peter Hawker, and between them they brought the flintlock to near perfection. Many locks were objects of fascinating ingenuity: waterproof locks, enclosed locks with smoke-vents, upside-down locks, locks with musical springs and elaborate safety-devices, etc. It was a time of confusing patent claims and counter-claims, summed up in the *New Patent Shooting Song* of 1817 which began:

'What lots of gun patents, tis wondrous I ween
We jolly old knights of the trigger have seen
Patent pans, patent hammers, and waterproof locks
Patent breeches and touchholes and patent-shap'd cocks'

But there was no disguising the fact that the flintlock had serious limitations. Apart from its susceptibility to damp there was a distinct pause between the ignition of the powder in the priming pan and that of the main charge; a pause during which the puff of smoke obliterated the target and alarmed any game.

Although scientists had been experimenting with the instantaneous detonating powers of fulminates – Samuel Pepys described the effects of gold fulminate in his *Diary* on 11 November 1663 – it was not until 1805 that the Scottish clergyman, Alexander Forsyth, invented his percussion lock using a form of detonating powder. The practical construction of the lock took place in the Tower of London in 1806 and its principle was patented in 1807. Then the new lock with its 'scent-bottle' magazine of percussion powder was successfully marketed. After some twenty uneasy years when other gunmakers had tried different types of percussion lock and Forsyth had sued any rival who he considered endangered his patent, the final percussion lock using a copper cap, developed by several makers, was generally adopted. All those intriguing breechloading and repeating actions that had defied the efforts of gunmakers to work properly with flintlocks now became possible. Within a few years the revolving pistol became the favourite personal arm.

English gunmakers like Robert and John Adams of London, Philip and James Webley and William Tranter of Birmingham produced well-finished revolvers by the traditional hand-made methods, but they and the whole English gunmaking trade received a severe jolt with the arrival of the American inventor Samuel Colt for the Great Exhibition of 1851. He displayed hundreds of machine-manufactured revolvers which lacked the finish of English pistols but were easier to make and cheaper in price. During the Crimean War, Colt's factory in London sold thousands of revolvers to the British forces. As the English gunmakers began slowly to convert to machine manufacture, the development of reliable metal cartridges in the 1860s meant further changes in design. American gunmakers, in particular Smith & Wesson (who held the rights of an important patent), Remington, and, of course, Colt, had all the encouragement of a vast home demand and few legal restrictions. In England the reverse was true, and only Webley & Scott survived in strength to match the foreign competition. Their robust revolvers, made in a wide range of pocket, police, military and target models, were sold all over the world.

At the end of the 19th century, the repeating pistol reached its ultimate conclusion with the invention of the automatic pistol. The great Continental and American factories turned their attentions to the new and deadly weapon, and from them came the Belgian Browning, the German Mauser and Walther, and the American Colt. In England, the Mars pistol made a brief but decided impact, and then only Webley & Scott's range of automatic pistols, never entirely satisfactory, were left. As a final blow to the English pistol, legal restrictions, so ineffectively introduced over 300 years before, were now enforced by a succession of Firearms Acts.

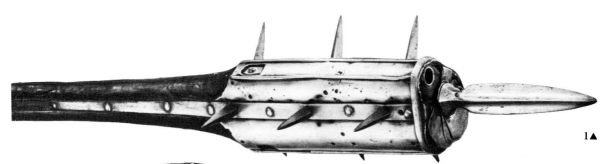

1 ▲

1. Two-handed club with spikes and a small spear. The head also contains three pistol barrels fired by hand-held match. The touch-holes originally had sliding lids, while swivelling plates covered the muzzles. This clumsy and dangerous weapon was described in the inventory of Henry VIII's armoury, taken after his death in 1547, as a Holy Water Sprinkler, but during the 17th century it became known as 'Henry VIII's Walking Staff'. (XIV.1)

2 ▲

3 ▼

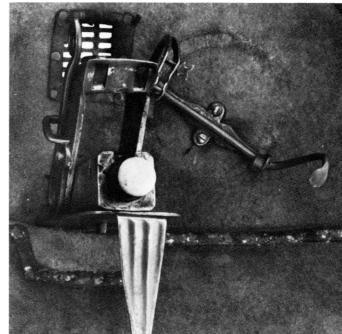

2. Pistol-shield from Henry VIII's armoury. Made of steel plates on a wooden base, it is armed with a breechloading, matchlock pistol. The shield was held by a grip in one hand, the other being employed to operate the matchlock which fired the pistol. Just above the barrel is a sighting aperture. A number of these pistol-shields were made during the 1540s, probably for Henry VIII's personal guard. (V.43)

3. Interior of the pistol-shield, showing the mechanism of the pistol. The breech could be opened for the insertion of a reloadable steel cartridge filled with powder and ball. The slow-burning match was held in a swivelling holder or serpentine, which brought the glowing end on to the touch-hole when the trigger or lever was pressed. Like most combination weapons, the pistol-shields were more impressive than practical.

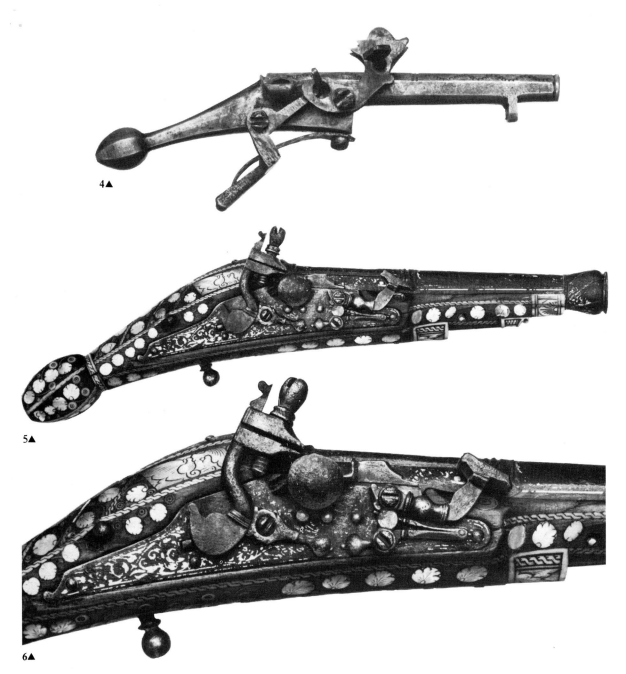

4▲

5▲

6▲

4. Elizabethan toy pistol. Made entirely of brass, the stock and barrel copy the shape of the contemporary wheellock and flintlock pistol. As either lock would be unpractical on a toy, a simple matchlock mechanism has been fitted. Similar toys have been found on several English archaeological sites, many in London. This pistol was found on the foreshore of the River Thames near the Tower of London. (XII.5235)

5, 6. One of the first decorated English pistols of about 1600, only a foot long, a type described in Holinshed's *Chronicles* as 'a pretty short snapper'. The walnut stock is inlaid with engraved bone and mother-of-pearl, while the metal parts are damascened with gold decoration. It is fired by a flintlock, then known as a snaphance, whose cock held a flint to strike sparks from a steel over the priming pan. (XII.1823)

7. Plain Civil War pistol of about 1645 with an English type of flintlock, in which the steel and pan-cover were combined. When the flint struck the steel the priming pan was automatically uncovered. Although simpler than the snaphance, the English lock still used the old complicated release or sear. To avoid accidental discharge, the trigger was protected by a guard and a dog-catch held the cock secure. (XII.1681)

8. 9. Pair of officer's holster pistols, made during the Commonwealth (1649–60). The 14in barrels have been tested at an official proof-house and bear its proofmarks, the arms of England and Ireland (St. George's Cross and a Harp). The locks are signed by the London gunmaker, William Watson, who was Master of the Gunmakers Company, 1645–7, and died in 1652. The ebony stocks have silver mounts engraved with floral ornament. (XII.1495-6)

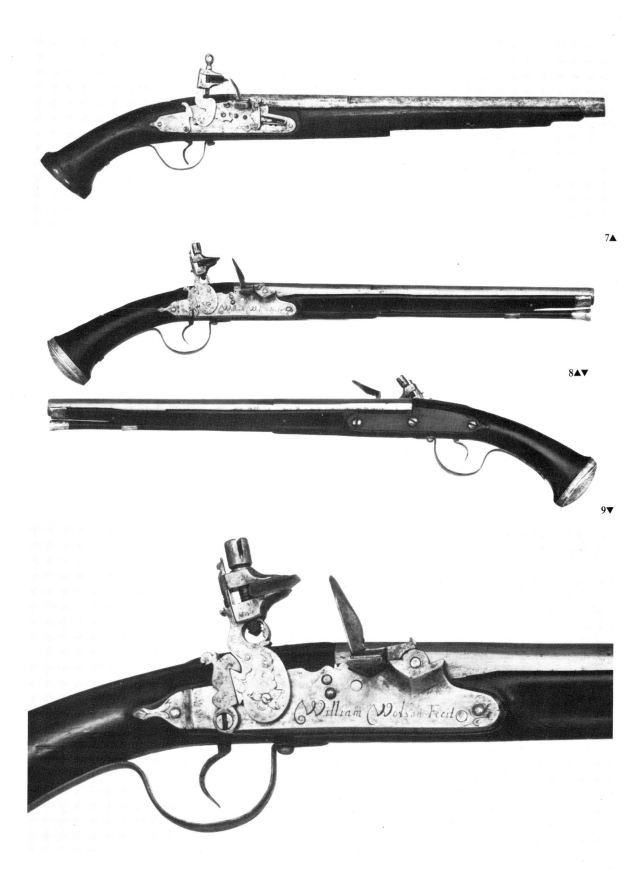

7▲

8▲▼

9▼

9

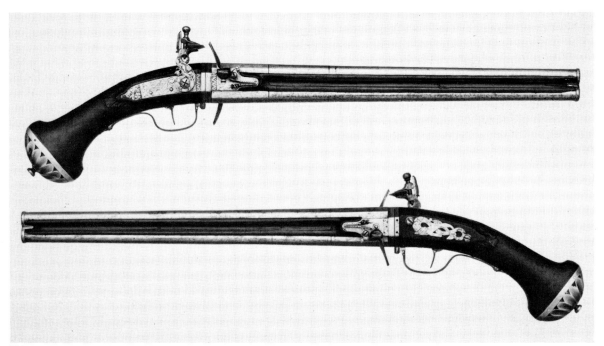

10▲

10. Pair of long double-barrelled flintlock pistols of about 1660. Each pistol has only one lock, but the 16in 'over-and-under' barrels are both equipped with pan and steel, and are turned over by hand to bring each in turn into the firing position. A telescopic rammer is contained in the butt. Made by the Royalist gunmaker Harman Barne, who, imprisoned during the Civil War, became Gunmaker-in-Ordinary to Charles II. (XII.4743–4)

11. Pair of flintlock pistols with rifled barrels. At this time most barrels were loaded from the muzzle, which was easy when they were smooth-bore but difficult when rifled. The barrels of these pistols could be unscrewed (one is shown) at the breech where the chamber was filled with powder and an oversize ball, which gripped the grooves of the rifling when fired. Made by an unknown English gunmaker, D. Wintle, about 1660. (XII.1497–8)

11▼

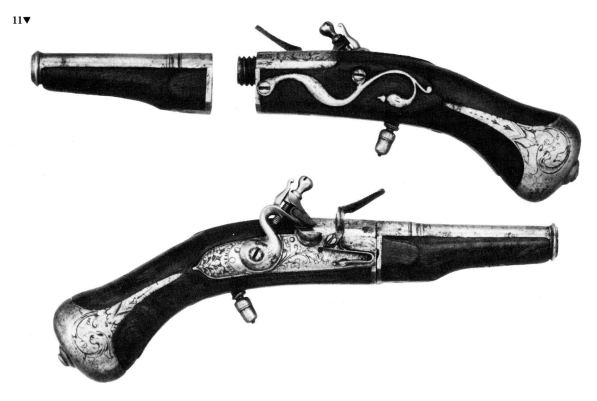

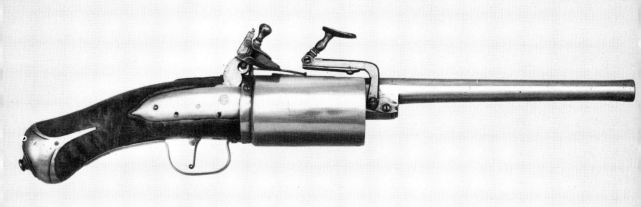

12▲

13▲

12, 13. English snaphance revolver with brass barrel, cylinder and mounts, about 1670. It was in advance of its time mechanically – pulling back the cock automatically revolved the six-chambered cylinder. This action was used by Samuel Colt who examined the pistol in 1851. But with its steel swivelled on the end of an arm and the pans uncovered by a push-rod, this was a clumsy and heavy (more than 6lb) pistol. (XII.1780)

14. Snaphance revolver by T. Annely, about 1710. Similar in design to No. 12 and with a brass barrel and cylinder, this pistol is just 12in long. The eight chambers are revolved in the same way by pulling back the cock, the next loaded chamber being positioned by a spring-catch. These early revolvers all suffered from misfires, and a nasty accident occurred if the chamber being fired was not in line with the barrel. (XII.4745)

14▼

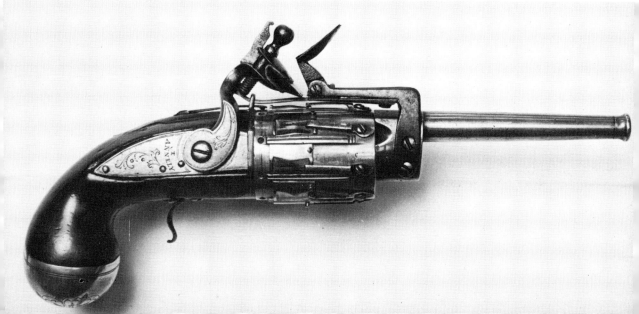

15▲   16▼

17▲ 18▼

15. Pair of holster pistols by Pierre Monlong, who was a French gunmaker, appointed to the Royal Household in Paris, 1664. For twenty years he supplied fine firearms to the royal and princely armouries of Europe. But, in 1684, he came to London as a Huguenot refugee. He was made 'Gentleman Armourer to his Majesty-in-Ordinary' in 1698, and these pistols may well have been made for William III. Monlong died in 1699 and was buried in the church of St. Martin-in-the-Fields. (XII.3829–30)

16–18. The steel barrels, locks and mounts of these Monlong pistols are chiselled and engraved with scrolls and foliage enlivened with grotesque masks and figures. The barrels are further damascened with gold scrolls. The walnut stocks are inlaid with delicately-cut silver sheet and wire in designs based on the pattern books published in Paris by Jean Bérain (1659), C. Jacquinet (1660) and Claude Simonin (1685). Made in London, about 1695, these are probably the finest examples of decorated English pistols surviving.

19, 20. After the Restoration in 1660, a 'Line of Kings' was displayed in the Armouries. Armours considered suitable for monarchs from William the Conqueror onwards were made realistic with carved wooden figures and mounted on wooden horses. When the effigy of William III was created after his death in 1694, his equipment included this pair of dummy pistols (without barrels and locks), the butt-caps cast with royal monograms (**20**). (XVI.3–4)

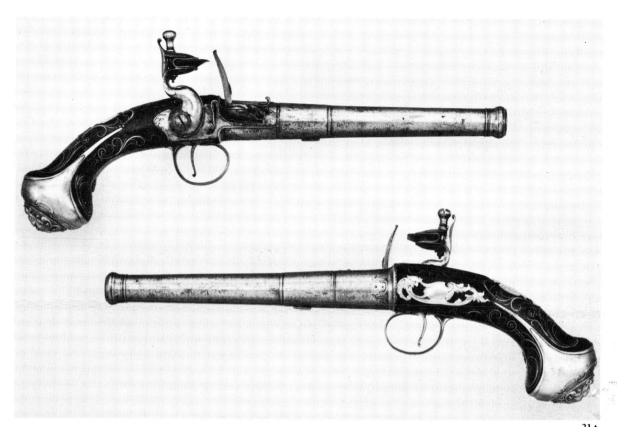

21A

21, 22. Pistols whose barrels could be unscrewed or 'turned off' for loading became popular in Georgian England. The cannon-shaped barrels were usually fitted with a lug underneath so that a spanner could be used for unscrewing. This pair of travelling pistols by William Turvey of London, who worked about 1715–40, have fine silver mounts, including a butt-cap with a grotesque mask (22), a characteristic feature of the period. (XII.1703–4)

23. Pair of pocket pistols by Richard Wilson, about 1780. By this date English gunmakers were making flintlock actions in metal boxes with the mainsprings extending inside the butts. Using this 'box-lock' construction, together with turn-off cannon-barrels which needed no rammers, gunmakers could make pistols small enough to be carried in a waistcoat pocket or a lady's muff. The barrels of these little silver-mounted pistols are only 2in long. (XII.1667–8)

◄22

23▼

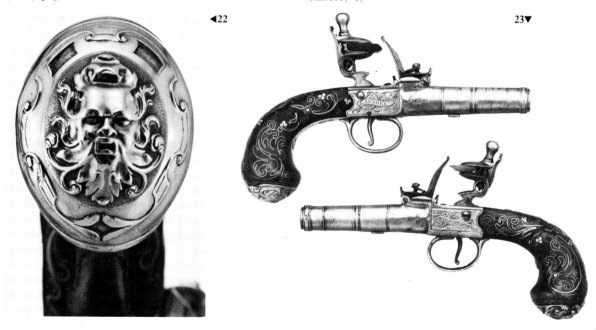

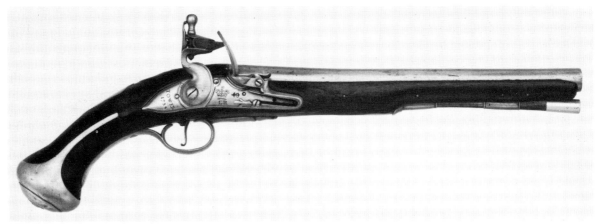

24▲

25▲   26▼

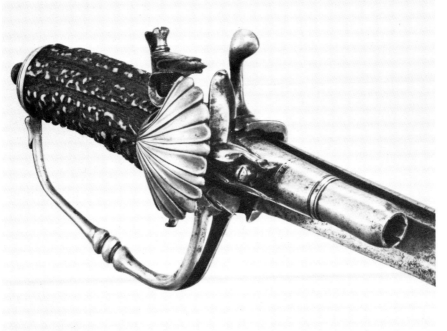

24, 25. Flintlock cavalry pistol, dated 1738. Designed for rough usage, but with a sturdy grace, this standard Heavy Dragoon pistol had a strong lock engraved with the royal monogram, G R. As the Tower of London was the headquarters of the Board of Ordnance, responsible for the supply of weapons, the lock is also marked TOWER. The 12in barrel, of carbine bore, bears the regimental marks 2D TROOP H G GDS [Horse Grenadier Guards]. (XII.806)

26. Combined sword and flint-lock pistol, about 1730. Bladed weapons like the spear and sword were sometimes fitted with a pistol for additional protection. This is a typical 18th-century English hunting-sword with a stag-horn grip and a silver hilt constructed to hold a small flintlock pistol. Made by Philip Vandebaize of London, it was probably intended to deliver a *coup de grâce* to an animal cornered by hounds. (XIV.24)

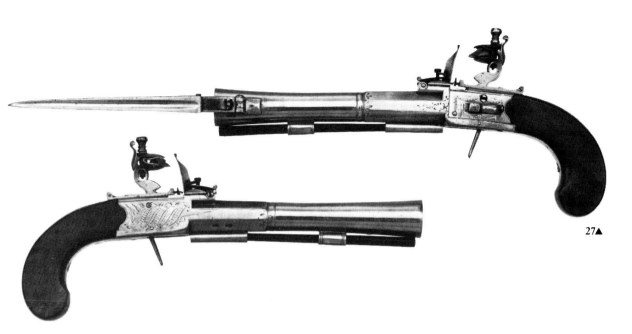

27. Pistols with brass barrels, resistant to rust, were the favourite arms of travellers in danger on land and sea. In case of misfire, they were often fitted with folding bayonets, which sprang into action at the touch of a button. This pair of brass-barrelled blunderbuss pistols was made by H. W. Mortimer of London about 1780 when the countryside was swarming with footpads and highwaymen. (XII.1717–8)

28. Flintlock belt-pistol of the early 19th century, marked simply LONDON. Pistols of this kind, with four splayed-out barrels, designed to fire a volley, were nicknamed 'duck's-foot' pistols. They were made in the assumption that four barrels were better than one when trying to stop the onrush of a mob. The turn-off barrels are notched at their muzzles so that a turn-key can be inserted for unscrewing. (XII.5079)

28▼

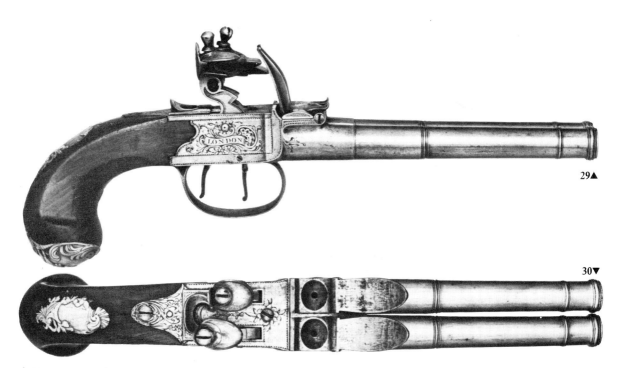

29, 30. With the ever-present chance of a misfire, pistols with more than one barrel were preferred. Too many barrels, however, meant too much weight, so that the double-barrelled pistol was most favoured. This silver-mounted pistol, one of a pair by Griffin & Tow of London, made about 1775, has two side-by-side barrels, each with its own flintlock, controlled by a sliding safety-catch and fired by a separate trigger. (XII.1709)

31, 32. This double-barrelled pistol is one of a pair made by Thomas Henshaw of London, with silver mounts hall-marked in Birmingham in 1776/7. It differs from No. 29 in having only one flintlock, the cock mounted centrally and the two adjoining pans covered by a wide steel. The left-hand pan has a sliding lid to protect the priming when the right barrel is fired. If necessary, both barrels could be fired together. (XII.1711)

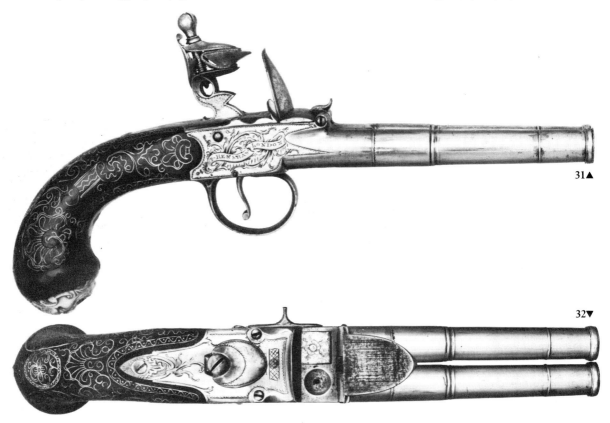

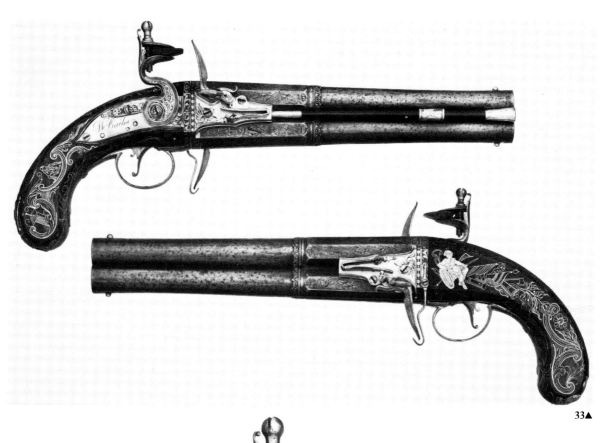

33▲

33, 34. Pair of flintlock holster pistols by William Bailes of London, about 1760. The double 'over-and-under' barrels of these pistols, each with its own priming pan and steel, turn over to be fired in turn by a single cock. While the actions are made with mechanical precision, the out-

34▼

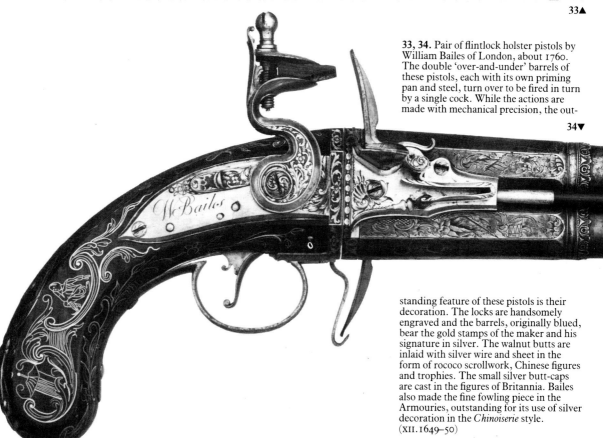

standing feature of these pistols is their decoration. The locks are handsomely engraved and the barrels, originally blued, bear the gold stamps of the maker and his signature in silver. The walnut butts are inlaid with silver wire and sheet in the form of rococo scrollwork, Chinese figures and trophies. The small silver butt-caps are cast in the figures of Britannia. Bailes also made the fine fowling piece in the Armouries, outstanding for its use of silver decoration in the *Chinoiserie* style. (XII.1649–50)

35▲   36▼

35–38. English gunmakers of the 18th century were noted more for the shooting qualities of their guns than their decoration, but there were a few whose artistic work rivalled that of the best French and German makers. One was Henry Hadley, who worked in London from about 1730 until his death in 1773. He specialised in silver-mounted pistols. This pair (**35**) is one of a series of which two pairs are in the Royal Collection, Windsor Castle. The locks are finely engraved with a scene of an angel and a cherub with books and instruments suggesting the Arts (**36**). They are fastened to the stocks by screws with square-socketed heads intended for a special screwdriver (**37**). The blued barrels are inlaid in gold with the maker's mark and imitation Spanish barrelmakers' marks. At this time Spanish gun barrels were renowned for their strength and beauty and were often used by English gunmakers. The touch-holes are also lined with gold, for protection against corrosion as well as decoration. On the walnut stocks are heavy silver mounts cast and chased with allegorical figures, classical busts and trophies. The escutcheon-plates on top of the butt bear the arms of the Dukes of Marlborough (**38**), possibly those of the 4th Duke, George Spencer (1739–1817), for whose coming-of-age in 1760 these pistols were perhaps made. (XII.1645–6)

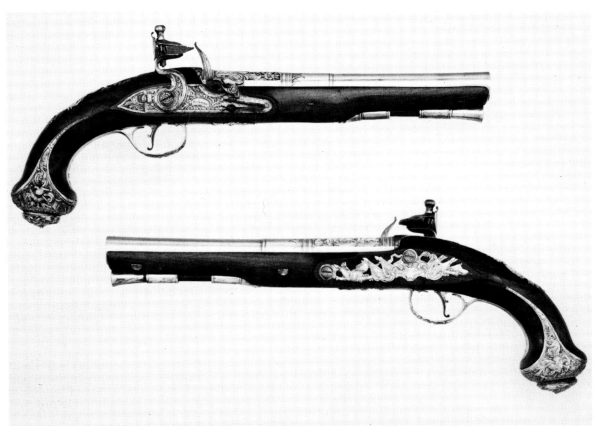

39▲   40▼

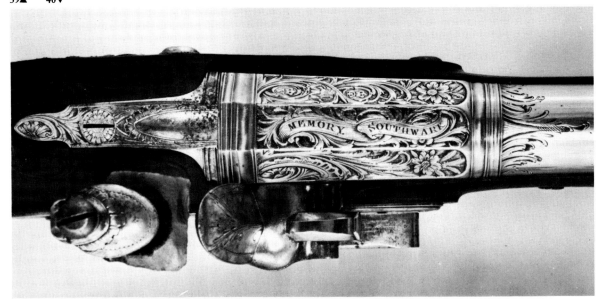

39, 40. English pistols at their best, combining utility with good looks. An example of the combined work of several craftsmen belonging to the craft Companies of the City of London. The cast and chased silver mounts (butt-caps, etc.) bear the London hallmarks for 1780/1 and the maker's mark of John King of the Goldsmith's Company. The engraving of the locks and barrels was probably executed by William Sharp of the Loriners' Company.

The gunmaker, Michael Memory, whose signature appears on the brass barrels, was apprenticed in the Gunmakers' Company at the age of 14, and after serving seven years was made freeman in 1743. His proof or trial piece was approved in 1749 when he was granted his own mark. This is stamped on the breech with the proof marks of the Gunmakers' Company of which he became Master in 1774. (XII.1657–8)

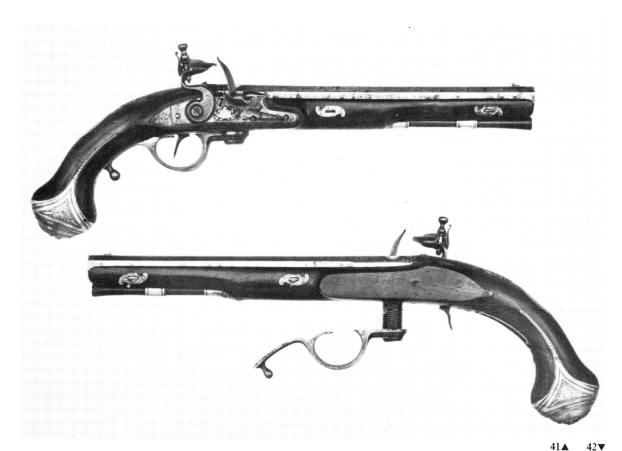

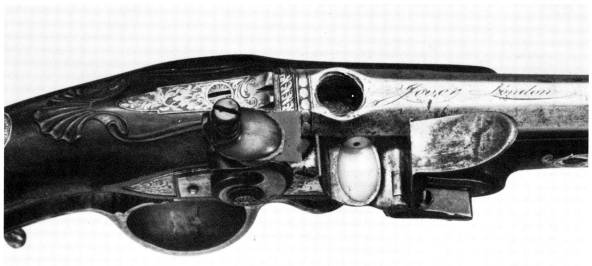

41▲ 42▼

41, 42. Many attempts were made to increase the speed of loading a gun, particularly when rifled. Various methods of opening the breech were tried, but with the loose powder and ball then in use these actions either jammed, broke down or simply took longer to operate than the ordinary method of muzzleloading. In 1776, the Scottish officer, Patrick Ferguson, patented an improved screwplug breech, opened by one turn of the trigger-guard. Ferguson demonstrated that his breechloading rifles could fire five shots a minute. Adopted briefly by the British Army, they became popular with sportsmen. A few pistols also used the breech. This rifled pair, one shown with the breech-plug unscrewed, were made by William Jover of London, about 1780. They have additional improvements like set or 'hair' triggers, anti-friction rollers on the lock-springs and sliding safety-catches. (XII. 1792 A-B)

23

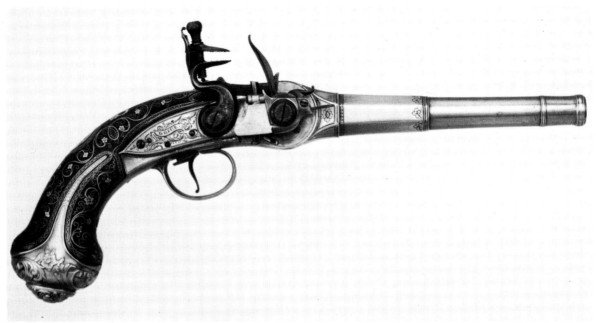

43▲   44▼

43, 44. Coupled with attempts to produce a workable breech-loader were experiments with multi-shot guns. Multi-barrelled guns – one English sportsman used one with 14 barrels – were too heavy; revolvers, whose priming pans and open chambers were difficult to keep dry, were rarely successful. An alternative was the repeating gun with separate magazines of powder and ball in the butt and an action bringing one charge at a time into the barrel. The magazine-gun relied on a complicated breech-mechanism, worked by a side-lever, which collected a charge of powder and a ball and fed them into the barrel, at the same time priming the flintlock. They were not only expensive to make, but often went wrong. This pistol, about 1780, has a brass action and barrel, and stock inlaid with silver decoration. Signed GRICE, LONDON, it was probably made in Birmingham. (XII.3835)

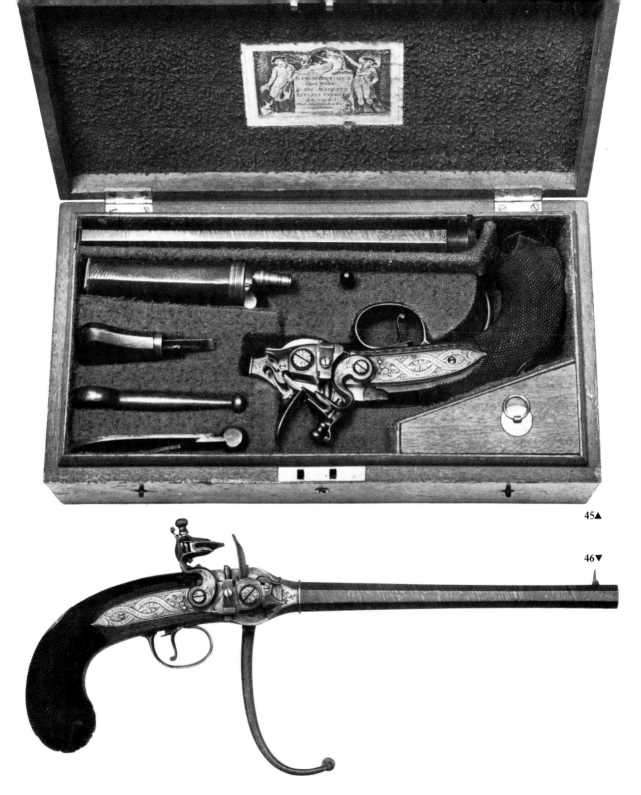

45, 46. Probably invented by Italian gunmakers in the 17th century and often named after one of them, Michele Lorenzoni of Florence, the magazine repeater was revived briefly by English gunmakers at the end of the 18th century. H. W. Mortimer, who made this pistol about 1795, became Gunmaker to George III in 1783. Famous for the creation of lavish gold-decorated guns, he also made a series of Lorenzoni-type repeating pistols. This is a rare cased example and is a masterpiece of artistic mechanism. Magazines in the butt carry enough powder and ball for seven shots. The green-felt lined mahogany case contains accessories for the pistol's maintenance – a red-leather covered powder-flask, a screwdriver and pricker, a wrench (to unscrew the barrel) and a bullet-mould. The case is engraved with the owner's name, Captain South, whose crest is on the pistol. (XII.4750)

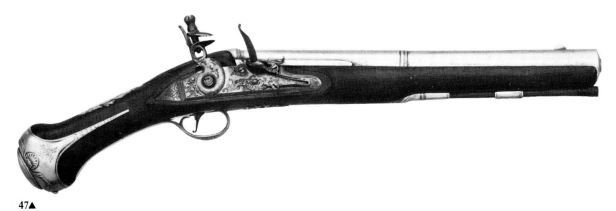

47▲

48▲   49▼

47-49. The uncertainty of fire from the flint-and-steel ignition of gunpowder led many gunmakers to put their faith in the airgun, which was untroubled by damp, never lacked for power, and had the advantage of being nearly noiseless. The first airguns of the 16th century relied on compressed air from bellows or a spring-piston, and had little power. By the 18th century, airguns, powerful enough for hunt or war, had built-in reservoirs filled with compressed air by a pump. This brass-barrelled pistol, made by Edward Bate of London, about 1770, has a tubular reservoir which encloses the barrel and is filled by a pump concealed in the butt (**48**). The compressed air was enough for several shots, a valve worked by a mechanism disguised as a flintlock releasing sufficient air for each shot. Many airguns and pistols were made like flintlocks, perhaps to create an element of surprise, and sometimes because, as silent killers, airguns were banned by law. (XII.3833)

50, 51. Another air pistol by Bate, with silver mounts hallmarked 1785. The lock, made as a flintlock, has an internal mechanism which opens the valve of an air reservoir in the shape of an iron ball. The ball-reservoir was unscrewed and filled by a separate pump, which meant that spare balls could be carried, but they were heavy and made the pistol – it weighs more than 4lb – unwieldy to use. Another advantage of the ball-reservoir was that it could be made interchangeable between pistol and rifle. Its force was often sufficient to discharge nearly 20 shots at ranges up to 100 paces, but it was difficult to gauge the right pressures; too little and the bullet had insufficient power, too much and the ball or the barrel burst. Then the airgun suddenly lost all its attractions. (XII.3834)

51▼

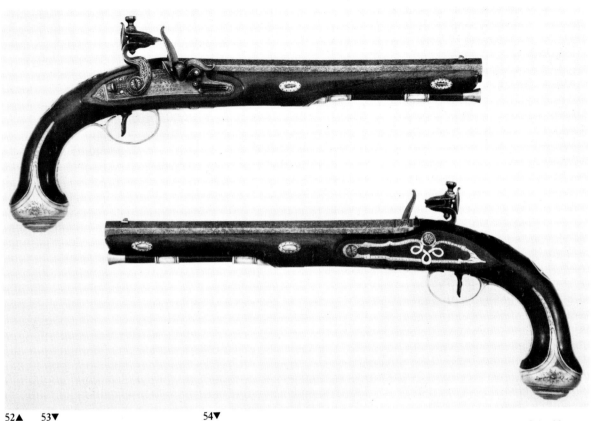

52▲ 53▼   54▼

52–54. Pair of fine pistols by John Manton, the elder of the two famous brothers, with silver mounts bearing London hallmarks for 1787/8. The flintlocks have all the refinements of the time: safety-catches, waterproof pans and springs with rollers. The patent breeches are also fitted (probably later) with platinum touch-holes, claimed by Joseph Manton as his invention. The escutcheon-plates (53) are engraved with the arms of Owen of Madoc. The barrels are also interesting. They are made with breech-plugs ending in a hook which clipped into a plate on the breech-tang. With these so-called 'false breeches' the barrels could be taken out easily without unscrewing. They are also made in the Damascus fashion, iron and steel bars being twisted and welded together to form a very strong tube with an attractive surface pattern (54), here emphasised by acid treatment. (XII.1733–4)

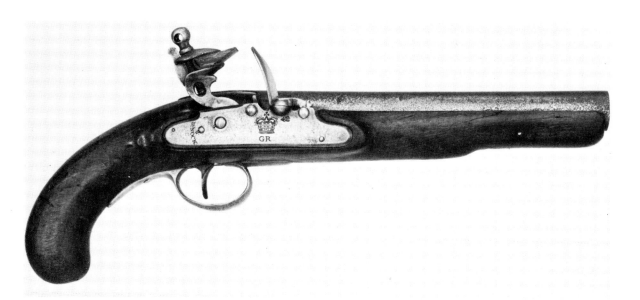

55, 56. Cavalry pistol of 1796 for the 2nd Dragoon Guards, with the screwless, enclosed flintlock invented by Henry Nock, the London gunmaker, in 1786. The flints, small moving parts and springs of any flintlock were liable to break. While the sportsman could mend his lock at leisure, the soldier in the field was dependent on the services of an armourer with special tools, and these were not always available. Nock's lock could be dismantled easily without tools. The new lock was adopted by the British Army and fitted to a new form of musket. A smaller version was made for pistols which were redesigned for the purpose with the minimum of fittings, the rammer being carried separate from the pistol. Nock's lock, which can be seen dismantled (56), performed well but proved too expensive and difficult to make and was soon replaced by a conventional pattern. (XII.1754; XII.3497C)

55▲ 56▼

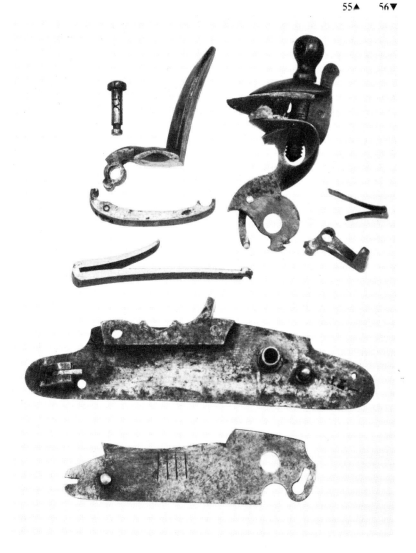

57.▲

57. Satirical cartoon of the duel between the Duke of Wellington (on the right) and the Earl of Winchelsea in 1829. It took place at Battersea Fields and was the result of a quarrel over the establishment of King's College, London. Both men, in fact, fired at random and honour was satisfied without bloodshed. In other duels, a man's life depended on the accuracy and 'feel' of his pistol.

58. Pair of flintlock duelling pistols with 'hair-triggers', by Robert Wogdon of London, about 1780. They were designed to fit the hand so that they became an extension of the arm. Some men fired instinctively as they pointed at the opponent, the sensitive triggers firing at a mere touch. Robert Wogdon had a poem, *Stanzas on Duelling*, dedicated to him in 1783. It began, 'Hail Wogdon, Patron of that leaden Death . . .' (XII.1369 A-B)

58.▼

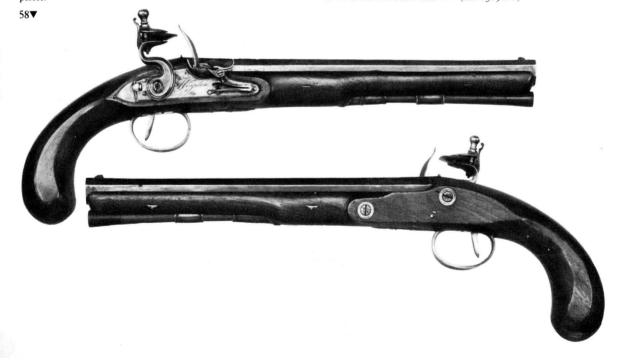

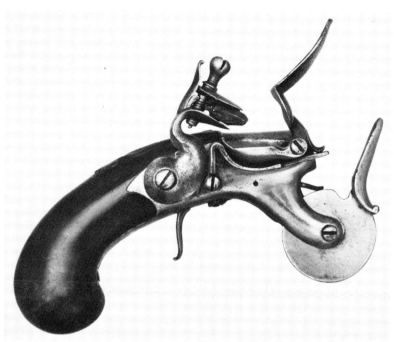

59. Gunpowder of the 17th and 18th centuries was often of uncertain quality and had to be tested before use. This brass powder-tester or eprouvette, like a pistol without its barrel, was made by T. Fletcher, about 1720. It fired a given charge of powder (without ball) against a sprung lid. The extent to which the lid was forced open indicated on a numbered wheel the strength of the powder. (XIII.162)

60. The accuracy of a pistol depended not only on the effectiveness of the lock and barrel and the strength of the gunpowder, but on the care with which it was loaded. Illustrated are the tools then considered necessary. They include a powder flask, the spout forming a measure; pincer bullet-mould; cloth or leather patches to wrap round the lead ball; and an assortment of screwdrivers, spring-lifters and cleaning jags. (XII.4746–9, 1484–5, 1532–3, 1735–6)

59▲   60▼

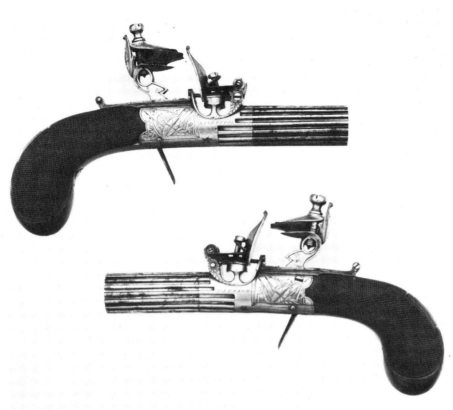

61. Most flintlock pocket pistols had turn-off barrels which needed a wrench. As such wrenches could be lost, the maker of this pair of pistols, about 1820, Patrick of Liverpool, has ribbed the barrels so that they can be unscrewed by hand. For ease of carrying, folding triggers – they spring out when the pistol is fully cocked – provide a smoother outline, while safety-catches secure the waterproof priming-pans. (XII.1722–3)

62. In 1792 an Act of Parliament established eight Police Offices in London. Policemen were well armed then and each Office purchased its own supply of cutlasses, truncheons, rattles, handcuffs and pocket pistols. The dealer who soon gained a monopoly of this trade was the gunmaker, William Parker of Holborn, London. He made this pair of pistols (only 5in long) in 1826. The brass actions are inscribed POLICE LAMBETH ST. (XII.1695–6)

61▲   62▼

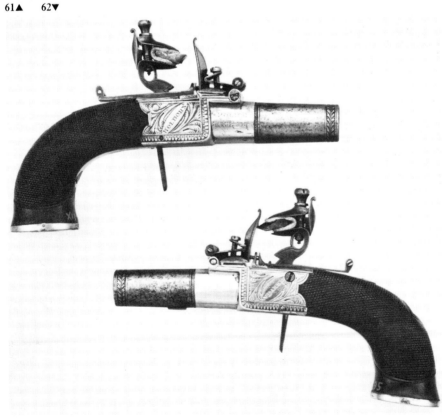

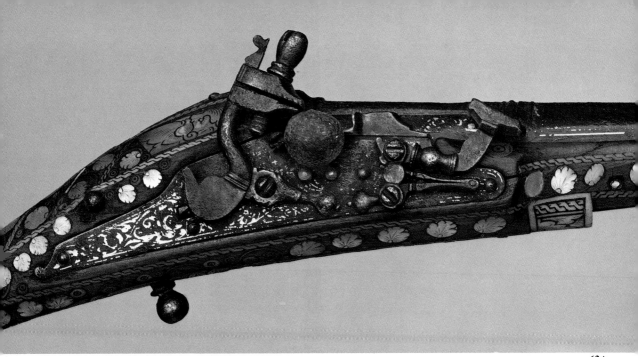

63. Close-up of the snaphance lock of the English pistol (see 5, 6), made about 1600. It is shown in the fired position with the steel thrust forward. Unlike the later flintlock, it could be carried cocked and loaded but was perfectly safe with the steel in this position. Note the comparatively crude inlay of engraved bone strips and plaques with mother-of-pearl discs. Traces of gold damascening can be seen on the locks. (XII.1823)

64. Close-up of the side-plate of one of the Monlong pistols (see 15–18) of about 1695. Gold scrolls are damascened on the barrel, which was originally blued. Much of the flowing scrollwork in chiselled steel and engraved silver inlay is based on the pattern book of Claude Simonin, published in Paris in 1685. The style of the rest comes from earlier designs by Jean Bérain (1659) and C. Jacquinet (1660). (XII.3829)

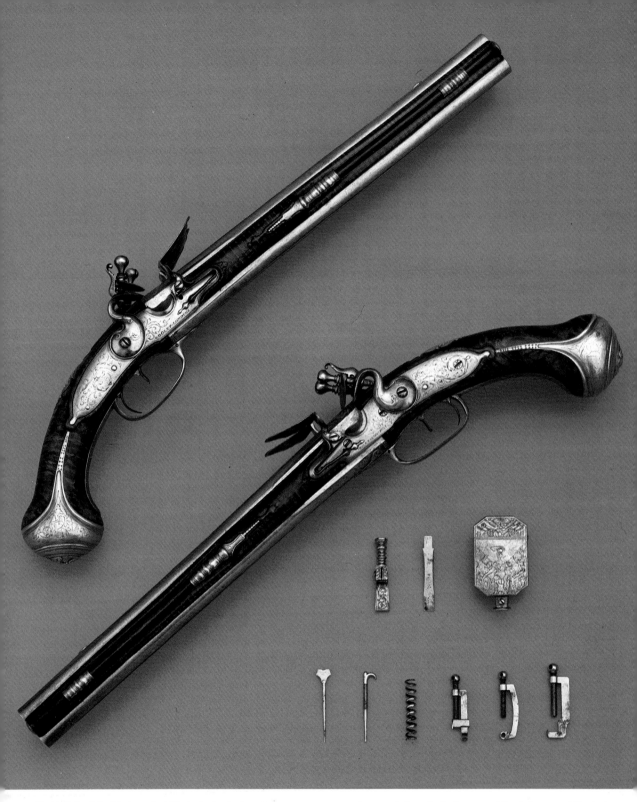

65, 66. Pair of double-barrelled flintlock pistols signed DOLEP LONDINI. Andrew Dolep, a Dutch gunmaker, who came to London about 1680, was made a freeman of the Gunmakers' Company in 1686 and was granted denization in 1691. His mark AD under a star is stamped on the barrels. Gunmaker to Prince George of Denmark, Consort of Queen Anne, Dolep produced several unusual pieces including a combined airgun and flintlock gun, and a superb fowling piece firing two superimposed charges, now in the Royal Armoury, Turin. The latter and the pocket set of gun tools shown (**66**), also by Dolep, bear the Medici arms. (XII.4517–8; XIII.192)

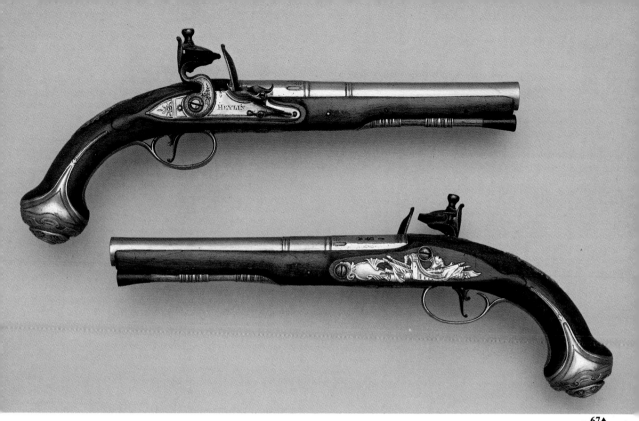

67. Pair of flintlock holster or travelling pistols by Joseph Heylin of Cornhill, London. He was elected freeman of the Gunmakers' Company in 1757, becoming their Master in 1777. Among his products were trade guns for the Hudson's Bay Company and the East India Company, fine pairs of pistols and at least one stone crossbow with a gun stock. These brass-barrelled and brass-mounted pistols are both colourful and practical. (XII.1699–1700)

68. Pair of flintlock pocket pistols with silver butts, the locks engraved LONDON, about 1750. English pistols became so popular that they were extensively copied in Liège, where they were known as *Pochettes à l'anglaise*. Nearly always of all-metal construction, they were marked 'London' or 'Segallas' after a family of London gunmakers. It is sometimes difficult to decide whether such pistols are English or Belgian copies. (XII.4513–4)

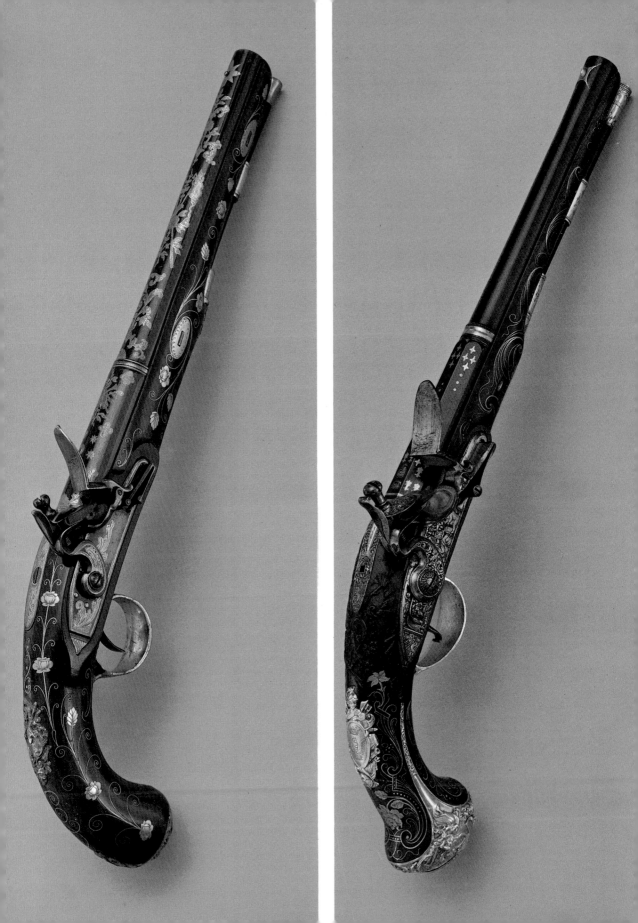

69, 70. One of a pair of flintlock pistols (see 101) made in
Birmingham for the export market, about 1830, compared with
(**70**) one of the pistols made by Henry Hadley (see 35–38), about
1760. Both are examples of the gunmaker's use of vivid blue and
gold decoration on the barrels and locks, set off by the purity of
the silver mounts and inlay on the stock. But whereas Hadley's
work is of the finest quality, the Birmingham product is a cheap
imitation; gilt finish instead of gold inlay, plated brass and alloy
replacing silver. (XII.1237; XII.1645)

◀◀**69** ◀**70**

71. The cased set of two pairs of John Manton pistols (see 89, 90),
made about 1804. A more restrained form of blue and gold
decoration has been used on these pistols, nicely contrasting with
the red leather-bound powder flask. Their case is lined with green
cloth forming a suitable background. The trade label on the case
describes John Manton as Gunmaker to the Prince of Wales and
the Duke of York. Not such a flamboyant character as his brother
Joseph, John was noted for the workmanship of his guns which
displayed ingenious mechanical features such as his single-trigger
action, patented in 1797. He was appointed Gunmaker to George
IV in 1831, and died three years later, aged 83. (XII.4746–9)

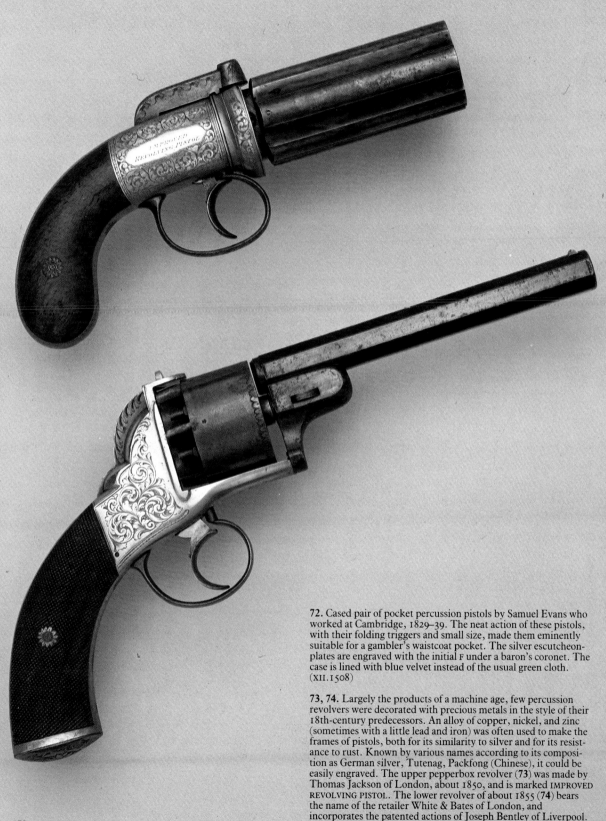

72. Cased pair of pocket percussion pistols by Samuel Evans who worked at Cambridge, 1829–39. The neat action of these pistols, with their folding triggers and small size, made them eminently suitable for a gambler's waistcoat pocket. The silver escutcheon-plates are engraved with the initial F under a baron's coronet. The case is lined with blue velvet instead of the usual green cloth. (XII.1508)

73, 74. Largely the products of a machine age, few percussion revolvers were decorated with precious metals in the style of their 18th-century predecessors. An alloy of copper, nickel, and zinc (sometimes with a little lead and iron) was often used to make the frames of pistols, both for its similarity to silver and for its resist-ance to rust. Known by various names according to its composi-tion as German silver, Tutenag, Packfong (Chinese), it could be easily engraved. The upper pepperbox revolver (73) was made by Thomas Jackson of London, about 1850, and is marked IMPROVED REVOLVING PISTOL. The lower revolver of about 1855 (74) bears the name of the retailer White & Bates of London, and incorporates the patented actions of Joseph Bentley of Liverpool. (XII.4151; XII.4164)

◀72 ▲73, 74

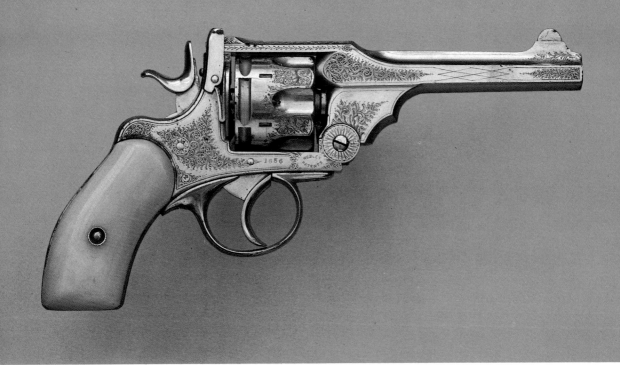

75▲

75, 76. Two examples of Webley & Scott centre-fire cartridge revolvers. The upper one (**75**) is the Mark III pocket model of .38in calibre, introduced in 1896/7. The butts of these revolvers are usually of walnut or bakelite, but this one, with a nickel-plated and engraved finish, is fitted with ivory grips. Top quality revolvers were gold-plated with mother-of-pearl grips. In 1904 Webley & Scott introduced the ws series of target and army

revolvers, calibred for the .455in cartridge (**76**). With a double-action, fast extraction and accurate barrels, such was their popularity among military and civilian marksmen that they were known as 'Bisley Target Revolvers'. This revolver has been cased and retailed by the Army & Navy Co-operative Society Ltd. in London. (XII.5238; XII.5237)

76▼

77. ▲

77. Multi-barrelled pistols firing single shots had to be provided either with several locks or with revolving barrels. A simpler method, introduced with the 'box-lock', was a priming-pan containing a revolving tap bored with touch-holes that could be directed to each barrel as required. This three-barrelled pistol by Smith of London, about 1815, has a tap-action which allows each barrel to be fired in turn or two together. (XII.3770)

78. Four-barrelled flintlock pistol by John Knubley, who worked in Charing Cross, London, about 1785–95. He was Gunmaker and Sword Cutler to the Royal Family and a contractor to the Board of Ordnance, supplying a wide range of arms from cannon locks to trade muskets. This ingenious brass-barrelled pistol has a German-silver tap-action so that the upper pair of barrels can be fired first, followed by the lower. (XII.1720)

78. ▼

79, 80. However much the flintlock was improved, its basic faults remained: it was susceptible to damp, its flint broke too often, and the puff of smoke from its priming-pan obscured the target and gave an alarm to game before the shot could take effect. In 1805, a Scottish clergyman, Alexander Forsyth (**79**), made a lock that used the detonating powers of fulminate or percussion powder to ignite the charge in a gun barrel. His lock (**80**) consisted of a swivelling magazine of percussion powder which deposited a small quantity in the touch-hole where it was detonated by a hammer replacing the flintlock's cock. His final experiments were conducted in the Tower of London in 1806. After failing to interest the military in his lock, he patented his invention in 1807 and started a gunmaking business to sell the new guns. (XVI.51)

79▲   80▼

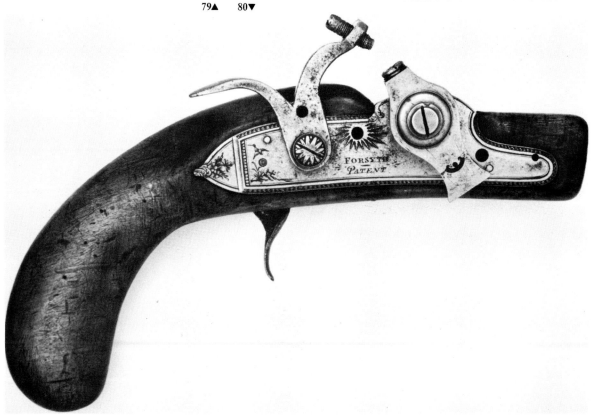

42

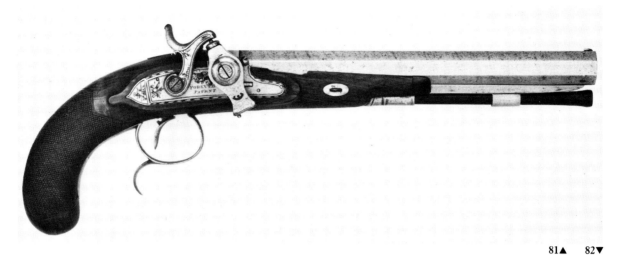

81▲   82▼

83▼

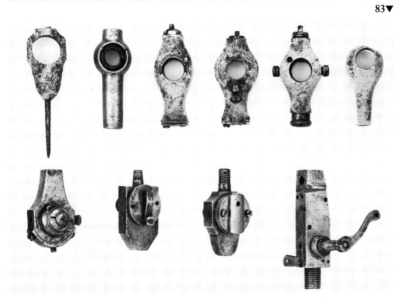

81–83. Forsyth's lock functioned well
when properly made and maintained, but
the loose powder was dangerous and
modifications were necessary. The pistol
(**81**), marked FORSYTH PATENT GUN COMPY
LONDON, was made about 1809 but had a
new magazine in 1810. A new type of
sliding magazine linked to the hammer was
designed for the later pistol (**82**), made in
1827. Some of Forsyth's experimental
pieces (**83**) indicate the difficulties of the
lock's construction. (XVI.51; XII.5006)

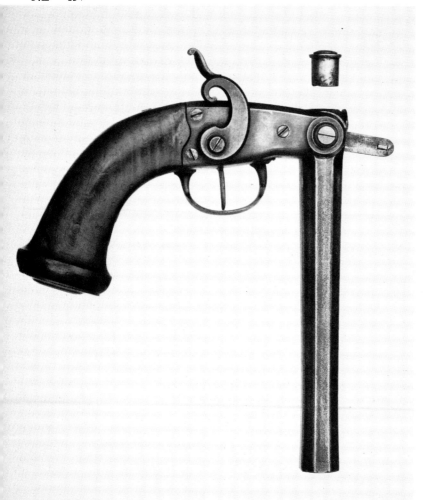

84, 85. The successful introduction of percussion locks encouraged gunmakers all over Europe to design new locks or actions. The Swiss inventor, Samuel Johannes Pauly (1766–1819?), patented in Paris, in 1812, a revolutionary breech-loading system employing a metal-based cartridge with a central percussion primer. He came to London and patented, in 1814, another type of lock for his breechloader, which used the heat of compressed air to ignite the cartridge. The top pistol (**84**), made about 1815, has a brass break-action breech with an outside cocking lever. A spring-loaded piston inside compresses air through a minute hole to fire the cartridge. The cartridge of the second pistol (**85**), shown next to the open breech, is set off by an internal hammer striking a percussion pellet in its base. Pauly also designed an airship called the Dolphin, but it never left the ground. (XII.4877; XII.3890)

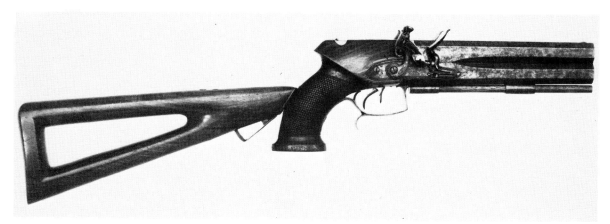

86▲   87▼

88▼

86, 87. Double-barrelled, 'over-and-under' flintlock pistol by the London gunmakers, Henry Tatham and Joseph Egg, who worked together in 1801–14. The pistol, weighing 3½lb, is shown with and without a clip-on skeleton stock which enabled it to be fired from the shoulder. It is marked TATHAM & EGG'S IMPROVEMENT. (XII.1380)

88. Flintlocks with external springs, which needed less cavity cut in the stock, were a speciality of Joseph Egg who made this pocket pistol, just 6in long. Its silver mounts bear London hallmarks for 1815/16 and the crest of an Earl of Aldborough. Egg made a similar pistol for George IV. (XII.1726)

89▲

89, 90. Cased set of a pair of duelling pistols and a pair of double-barrelled pistols by John Manton, about 1804. Both pairs of pistols are decorated *en suite*, i.e., with the same style of ornament. The browned Damascus barrels and blued locks are inlaid with gold trophies and the name of the maker (**90**). The touch-holes and priming-pans are also covered with gold. The pistols are in the best tradition of English gunmaking – restrained but handsome decoration allied to superb mechanical features. The barrels are cut with faint grooves known as 'secret' rifling; the locks of the double-barrelled pistols are set off in turn by two pressures on the single trigger. The locks are also unusual in having French-style 'spur' cocks. The brass-mahogany case bears the crest and motto of the owner, George Baring, Esq. (XII.4746–9)

90▼

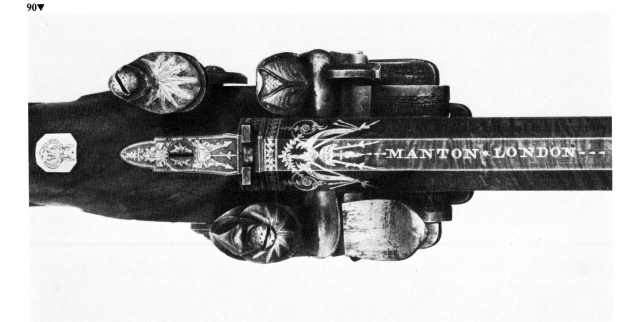

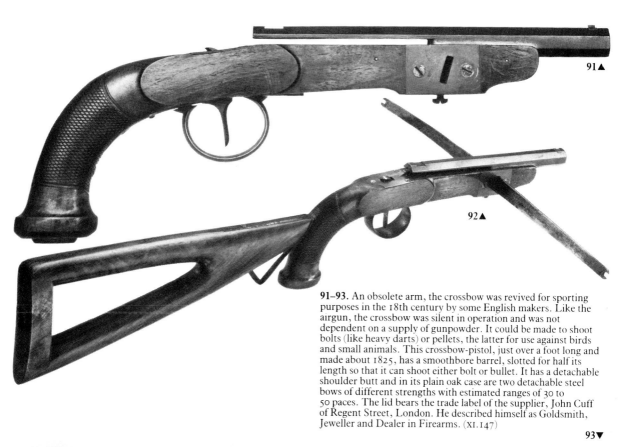

91▲

92▲

91–93. An obsolete arm, the crossbow was revived for sporting purposes in the 18th century by some English makers. Like the airgun, the crossbow was silent in operation and was not dependent on a supply of gunpowder. It could be made to shoot bolts (like heavy darts) or pellets, the latter for use against birds and small animals. This crossbow-pistol, just over a foot long and made about 1825, has a smoothbore barrel, slotted for half its length so that it can shoot either bolt or bullet. It has a detachable shoulder butt and in its plain oak case are two detachable steel bows of different strengths with estimated ranges of 30 to 50 paces. The lid bears the trade label of the supplier, John Cuff of Regent Street, London. He described himself as Goldsmith, Jeweller and Dealer in Firearms. (XI.147)

93▼

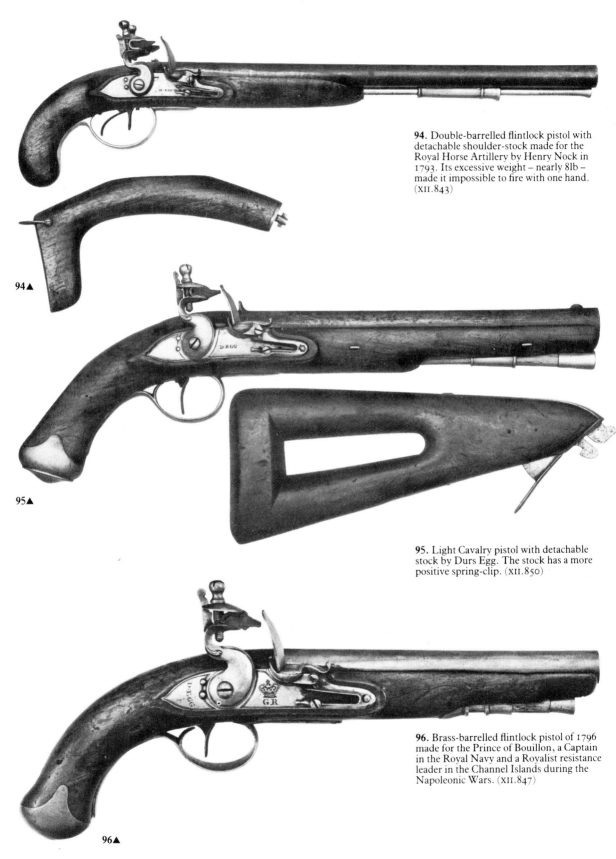

94. Double-barrelled flintlock pistol with detachable shoulder-stock made for the Royal Horse Artillery by Henry Nock in 1793. Its excessive weight – nearly 8lb – made it impossible to fire with one hand. (XII.843)

94▲

95▲

95. Light Cavalry pistol with detachable stock by Durs Egg. The stock has a more positive spring-clip. (XII.850)

96. Brass-barrelled flintlock pistol of 1796 made for the Prince of Bouillon, a Captain in the Royal Navy and a Royalist resistance leader in the Channel Islands during the Napoleonic Wars. (XII.847)

96▲

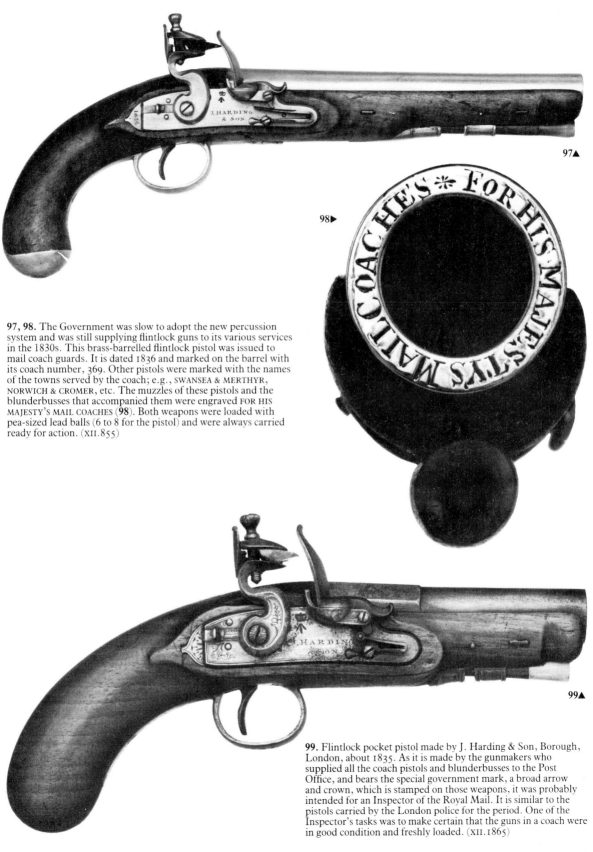

97, 98. The Government was slow to adopt the new percussion system and was still supplying flintlock guns to its various services in the 1830s. This brass-barrelled flintlock pistol was issued to mail coach guards. It is dated 1836 and marked on the barrel with its coach number, 369. Other pistols were marked with the names of the towns served by the coach; e.g., SWANSEA & MERTHYR, NORWICH & CROMER, etc. The muzzles of these pistols and the blunderbusses that accompanied them were engraved FOR HIS MAJESTY'S MAIL COACHES (**98**). Both weapons were loaded with pea-sized lead balls (6 to 8 for the pistol) and were always carried ready for action. (XII.855)

99. Flintlock pocket pistol made by J. Harding & Son, Borough, London, about 1835. As it is made by the gunmakers who supplied all the coach pistols and blunderbusses to the Post Office, and bears the special government mark, a broad arrow and crown, which is stamped on those weapons, it was probably intended for an Inspector of the Royal Mail. It is similar to the pistols carried by the London police for the period. One of the Inspector's tasks was to make certain that the guns in a coach were in good condition and freshly loaded. (XII.1865)

100▲

100. Flintlock revolver marked E. H. COLLIER LONDON 25 PATENT. Collier was an American engineer who patented his revolver in London in 1818. A few hundred sporting guns and pistols were made about 1820–30. The cylinder is turned manually, but there is a linked automatic priming magazine. Probably the last attempt to make a workable flintlock revolver, it was soon made obsolete by the percussion system. (XII.4000)

101▼

101. Pair of flintlock holster pistols made in Birmingham, about 1830, for the Eastern market. The barrels and locks are blued and decorated with gilt designs of trophies and a crescent surrounded by stars. The stocks are inlaid with a pattern of flowers and foliage in German silver. The mounts are of silver-plated brass. A cheap copy of the flamboyant pistols sometimes presented to Eastern potentates. (XII.1237–8)

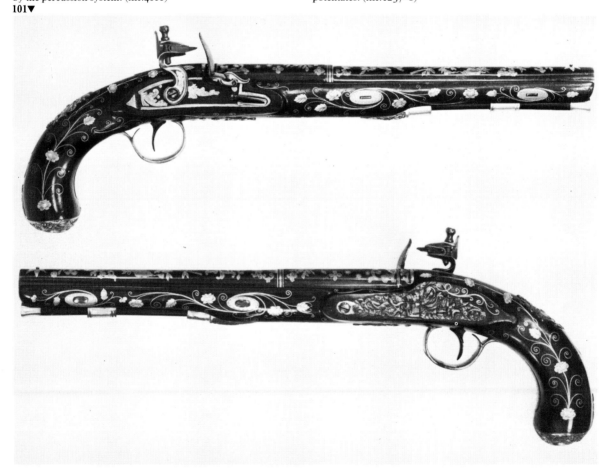

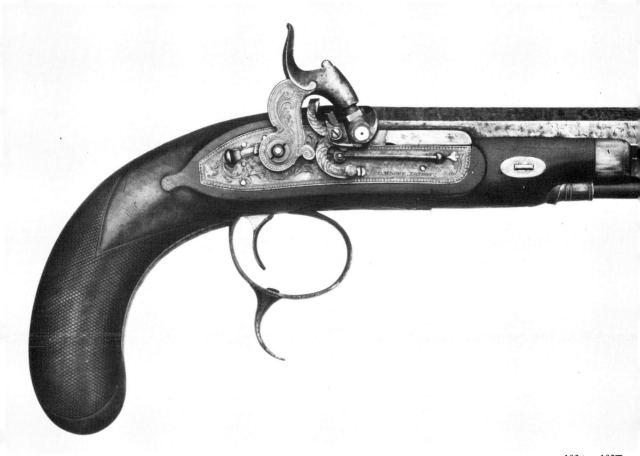

102. Forsyth's percussion lock with its powder-magazine primer was a great improvement on the flintlock but, if mishandled, could easily explode. Other gunmakers experimented with locks in which the percussion primer was in the form of pills, discs, tubes or tapes. This is a pill-lock by Charles Moore of London, about 1825. The pill was held in a nipple on the barrel and covered until ready to be detonated by the hammer. (XII.1538)

103. The percussion primer adopted by most gunmakers was a small copper cap with the detonating composition inside the crown which fitted over the barrel nipple. Gun locks became much simpler. In 1825 Isaac Riviere of London patented the percussion-cap lock shown here. It had only four parts and two springs and only the hammer was visible. Riviere described himself as the 'Patentee for the Guns without Locks'. (XII.1461)

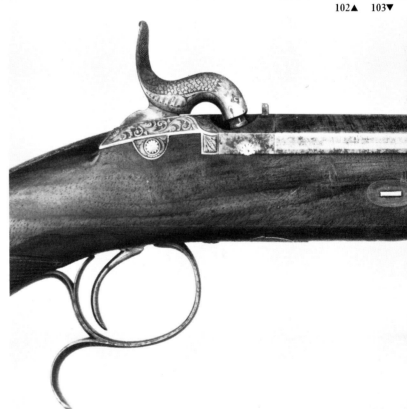

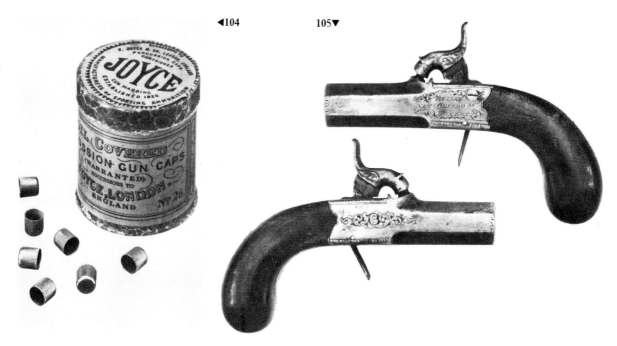

104-106. The manufacture of anti-corrosive percussion-caps was perfected by the London chemist, Frederick Joyce, and they were soon readily available in their distinctive bags and tins (**104**). Gunmakers could now design very small pistols and fit them to a variety of other weapons (swords, spears, knives), articles of wear (belts, walking-sticks) and household articles (door locks, burglar alarms). The pair of pistols (**105**) made by E. M. Reilly, New Oxford Street, London, are 4in long but fire a comparatively large ball of .57in calibre. They were the English equivalent of the American Derringer pistols. The sword-pistol (**106**) was made by the London sword cutler, Joshua Johnston, who has fitted a Birmingham-made percussion-cap pistol into the grip. (XX.929; XII.1518–9; XIV.25)

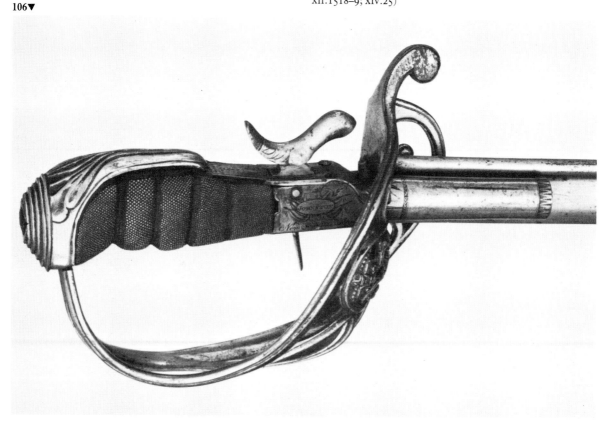

107▲

107. The percussion-cap lock revolutionised the design of revolvers. At first, gunmakers made pistols with a revolving cluster of barrels which, from their frontal appearance, earned them the nickname of 'pepperboxes'. This pepperbox pistol with folding trigger and conventional hammer by Samuel Nock of London, about 1830, has seven rifled barrels revolved by hand. Later models were 'self-cocking' and could be fired as fast as the trigger was pulled. (XII.5015)

108. A favourite pocket weapon of the 1840–50s was the combined percussion pistol and pocket knife. A dagger blade was included and the handle contained a bullet mould and pair of tweezers. These combination arms were nearly all made by the Sheffield cutlery firm of Unwin & Rodgers who, in their advertisements, claimed that their 6in-long 'Life and Property Preserver' could kill at 50 yards. (XIV.27)

108▼

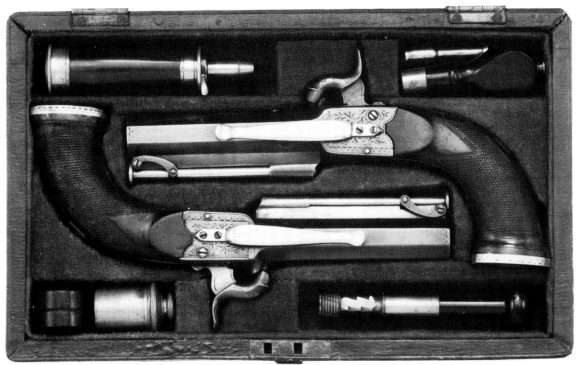

109▲

109–111. A cased pair of percussion belt pistols with folding triggers and swivel rammers (**109, 110**). The barrels are inscribed GERDINGS INVENTION. The case, which contains a powder flask, nipple-key, oil-bottle, cap-box and cleaning tools, is covered with dark red morocco leather stamped in gold with the royal monogram GR IV. This monogram is also engraved on the silver escutcheon-plates, while the flat butt-ends bear the royal crest in silver (**111**). George IV started collecting fine weapons, both contemporary and antique, when he was Prince of Wales. A special armoury was built in Carlton House and formed the basis of the Royal Armoury now at Windsor Castle. Augustus Gerding, a Hanoverian huntsman, served as Curator of the Royal Armoury from 1821 until retirement in 1866. His 'invention' appears to be a safety modification to the locks. (XII.1790 A-B)

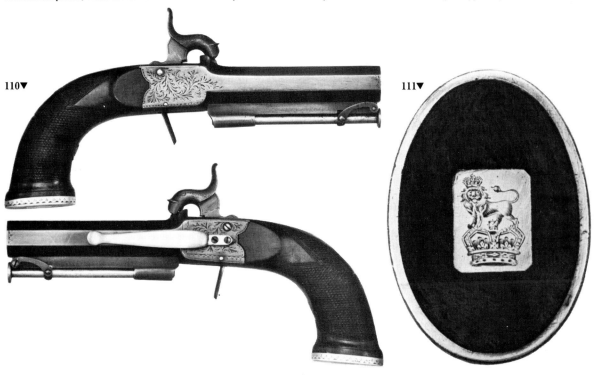

110▼

111▼

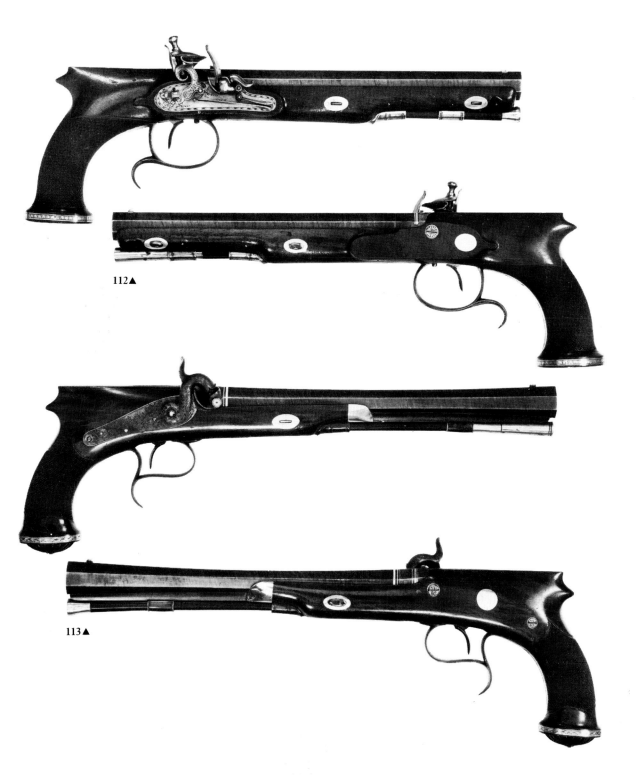

112▲

113▲

112, 113. The change-over from flintlock to percussion-cap lock is well illustrated by these two pairs of duelling pistols, both made by the same family of gunmakers, the Patricks of Liverpool. The flintlock pair (**112**) was made about 1810 by Jeremiah Patrick, gunmaker to the Duke of Gloucester. The locks have a single external spring serving both cock and steel, and are fitted with safety-catches. They are fired by hair-triggers. Whereas the flintlocks have full-length stocks, the percussion pistols (**113**) have short fore-ends. Both pairs are notable for the shape of their butts, known today as 'saw-handled' butts. They emphasised the line of the barrel extending straight along the extended arm. Probably made by Ann Patrick about 1830, the percussion locks are of the new back-action type with their springs, etc., behind the hammer. (XII.1727–8; XII.1735–6)

114▲

114, 115. In 1837 the American inventor J. W. Cochran patented in England a novel form of percussion revolver, with a hand-revolved flat cylinder in which the chambers were bored out like the spokes of a wheel. The hammer and trigger were underneath. This revolver had several advantages over the conventional pattern, foremost being the speed with which an empty cylinder could be replaced by a loaded one. But it was comparatively slow

to operate and a nasty accident could occur if the rear- or side-pointed chambers caught premature fire. Nevertheless, the London gunmakers Wilkinson & Son (in business today as Wilkinson Sword) made about seventeen guns and pistols under the patent in 1839–41. The seven-shot pistol illustrated was used by Lord Egerton (1806–59), sportsman, author and poet, on an expedition to the Near East. (XII.3899)

115▼

116. More than one shot could be fired from a barrel by loading it with superimposed charges. These could be set off like a Roman Candle firework or ignited one at a time by a sliding lock. Well known as early as the 17th century, the system was nevertheless patented by Jacob Mould in England in 1825. This four-shot pistol, about 1830, was made by the royal gunmaker, William Mills of London. (XII.1864)

117. One disadvantage of the percussion-cap lock was the diffi-culty in handling the small copper caps, particularly in cold weather. Some sportsmen carried them in pocket containers that dispensed one cap at a time. Westley Richards, the Birmingham gunmaker, patented this pistol with a self-capping device in 1838. The tubular magazine on the side of the barrel was pulled towards the lock where a cap dropped on to the nipple. (XII.3543)

117▼

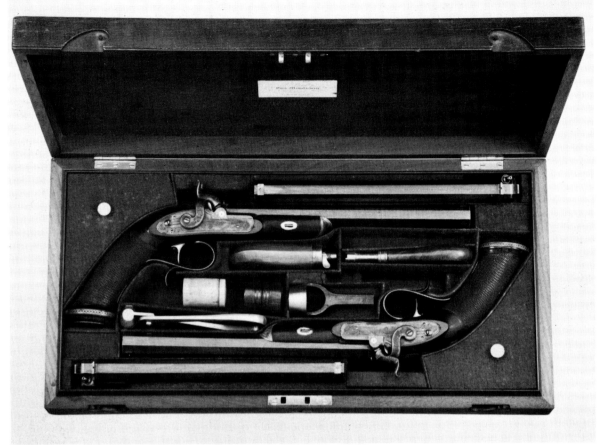

118. The plain, double-barrelled pistol with its sure action was favoured by many sportsmen. This pair of percussion pistols, each with one barrel smoothbore and the other rifled, was made in 1834 by James Purdey, the founder of the modern firm, famous for its shotguns. The mahogany case has a full set of accessories including turned-bone boxes for greased patches and spare nipples. Owned originally by Earl Canning. (XII.1530–1)

119. One of a pair of double-barrelled percussion pistols with folding bayonets, made about 1830 by George Wilbraham of London, who started his career as a gun viewer for the East India Company and was both gunmaker and sword cutler. The bayonet folds under the barrels where it is held by the trigger-guard which slides back to release it. An arrangement which necessitates the rammer being housed on the left side of the barrels. (XII.1394)

118▲

119▼

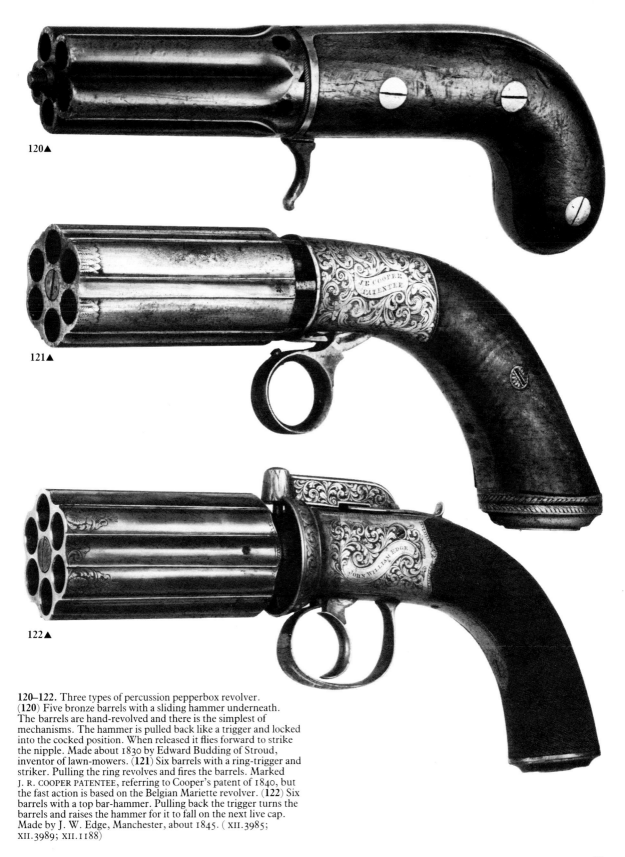

120–122. Three types of percussion pepperbox revolver. (**120**) Five bronze barrels with a sliding hammer underneath. The barrels are hand-revolved and there is the simplest of mechanisms. The hammer is pulled back like a trigger and locked into the cocked position. When released it flies forward to strike the nipple. Made about 1830 by Edward Budding of Stroud, inventor of lawn-mowers. (**121**) Six barrels with a ring-trigger and striker. Pulling the ring revolves and fires the barrels. Marked J. R. COOPER PATENTEE, referring to Cooper's patent of 1840, but the fast action is based on the Belgian Mariette revolver. (**122**) Six barrels with a top bar-hammer. Pulling back the trigger turns the barrels and raises the hammer for it to fall on the next live cap. Made by J. W. Edge, Manchester, about 1845. (XII.3985; XII.3989; XII.1188)

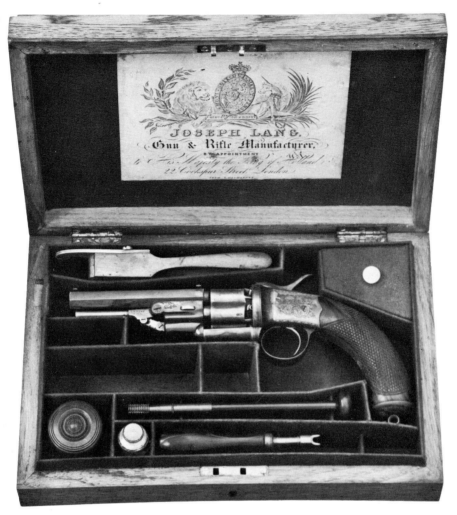

123. Pepperbox revolvers with their multiple barrels became too heavy when made in large calibres. In the 1850s gunmakers turned to revolvers with one barrel and a cylinder of chambers which could be loaded with prepared paper cartridges of ball and powder. This is a cased percussion revolver by Joseph Lang, London, fitted with a rammer patented by Pryse & Cashmore in 1855. The bullet mould produced both round and conical bullets. (XII.1465)

124▼

124. Percussion revolver inscribed HARVEY'S PATENT BREECH LOADING REVOLVING PISTOL. In 1853/4, W. J. Harvey, an Exeter gunmaker, took out patents for a hammerless self-cocking revolver. It had a firing-pin (or 'discharging-ram' as Harvey called it) acting parallel to the barrels, and an ingenious detachable rammer which also served as turnscrew and nipple-key. Probably made in Birmingham, the barrel has an unusual anti-clockwise rifling. (XII.1371)

125. James Webley was the elder of two brothers, both Birmingham gunmakers and revolver designers. James's revolvers were single-action, being cocked and revolved by thumbing back the 'long-spur' hammer. Patented in 1853, they were made in three sizes for holster, belt and pocket. Firing a 'Minié' bullet, this holster model had a range of 300 yards. James died in 1856, leaving the development of revolvers to his brother Philip. (XII.3918)

126. Two other brothers, Robert and John Adams of London, became famous for their revolvers. Robert patented his 'solid-frame' revolver in 1851 and established the London Armoury Company, which made this pistol in 1856. This Army Model has the double-action (cocked by a hammer or trigger) patented by Lieut. J. B. E. Beaumont in 1855. It was made for Maj. Gen. Sir L. V. Swaine, then an officer in the Rifle Brigade. (XII.1479)

126▼

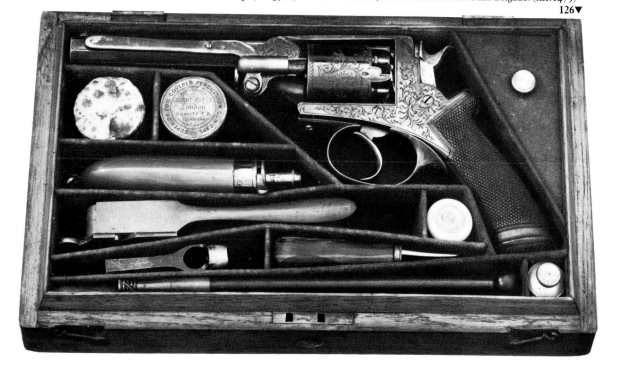

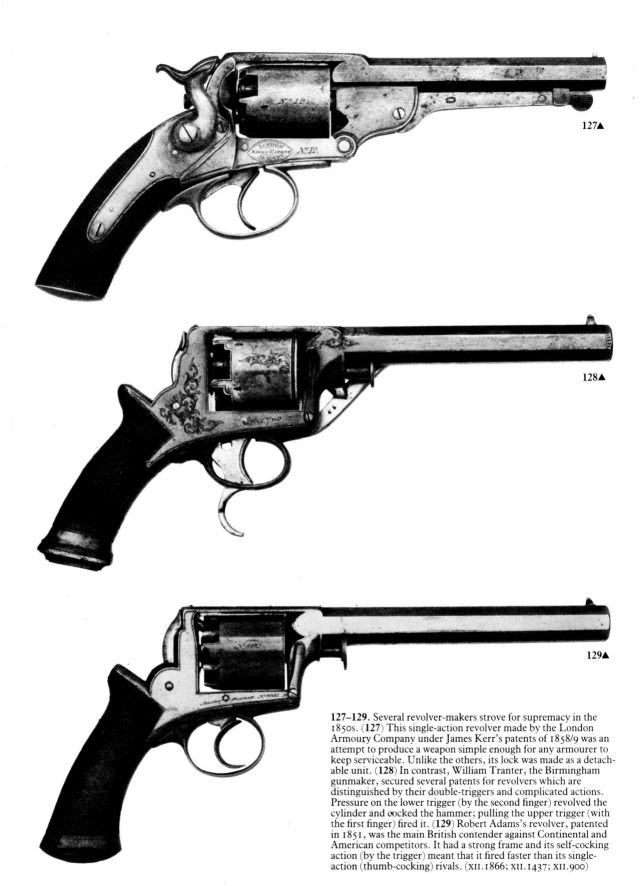

127–129. Several revolver-makers strove for supremacy in the 1850s. (**127**) This single-action revolver made by the London Armoury Company under James Kerr's patents of 1858/9 was an attempt to produce a weapon simple enough for any armourer to keep serviceable. Unlike the others, its lock was made as a detachable unit. (**128**) In contrast, William Tranter, the Birmingham gunmaker, secured several patents for revolvers which are distinguished by their double-triggers and complicated actions. Pressure on the lower trigger (by the second finger) revolved the cylinder and cocked the hammer; pulling the upper trigger (with the first finger) fired it. (**129**) Robert Adams's revolver, patented in 1851, was the main British contender against Continental and American competitors. It had a strong frame and its self-cocking action (by the trigger) meant that it fired faster than its single-action (thumb-cocking) rivals. (XII.1866; XII.1437; XII.900)

130–133. The man who had most influence on the design of revolvers and revolutionised the gunmaking trade was the American inventor, Samuel Colt (**130**). He patented his first single-action revolver as early as 1835, but it was an improved model, patented in 1849, that he brought to London for the Great Exhibition of 1851; not one, but hundreds, and all made by machinery with interchangeable parts. It was Colt's process of manufacture, so different from the traditional English hand-made methods, that created such an impression. He established a factory on the Thames at Millbank, which from 1853 until its closure in 1856 supplied thousands of his Navy Model (.36in calibre) revolvers to the British forces in the Crimean War. (**131–133**). This Navy Model pistol, shown from the top, the side and underneath was made and handsomely engraved in London. (XII.1434)

131▲

132▲   133▼

134▲

134–136. Percussion revolvers like the Colt and Adams used self-consuming paper or skin cartridges loaded into the front of the chambers. Continental and American gunmakers experimented with metallic cartridges, which could be quickly inserted from the rear and easily ejected. The pin-fire cartridge, with a detonator in its base fired by an upright pin, was invented by the French gunmaker, Lefaucheux, in 1835. Other French gunmakers designed cartridges with the priming in the rim or in the centre of the base. English revolvers were adapted to take these cartridges. (**134**) Cased rim-fire revolver by William Tranter, Birmingham, about 1865. Made for the Duke of Connaught; presented by George VI. (**135**) Gold-plated pin-fire revolver with ivory grips. Belgian design but probably made in Birmingham, about 1860. (**136**) Four-barrelled rim-fire pocket pistol, with revolving striker. Sharps's 1859 American patent pistol made by Tipping & Lawden, Birmingham, about 1865. (XII.1191; XII.4794; XII.4149)

137–139. Pistol designers were now faced with the problem of extracting the new metallic cartridges from the cylinder after firing. This could be done by a simple push-rod, one at a time; other ingenious mechanisms extracted all the cartridges at once. (**137**) Galand & Somerville's revolver patented in 1868, made in Birmingham and retailed by Henry Holland, London. Pulling the side-lever moved the barrel and cylinder forward leaving a plate-extractor with spent cartridges behind. (**138**) T. Thomas revolver, patented 1869. Made in Birmingham and retailed by Wilkinson, London. With the aid of the knob, the barrel is turned over, moving it and the cylinder forward, a stationary star-shaped extractor holding the empty cases. (**139**) Unusual 'hammerless' double-trigger (one for revolving, one for firing) revolver made by Kynoch Gun Factory, Birmingham, about 1890. It used the 'break-action' extractor system most popular in England. Opening the breech and bending the barrel down, made the extractor push all the cases out together. (XII.4890; XII.4098; XII.4907)

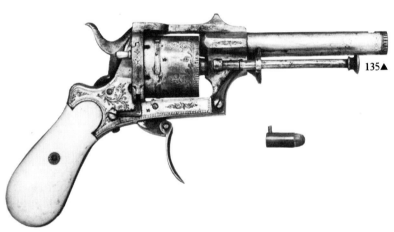

135▲

136▲

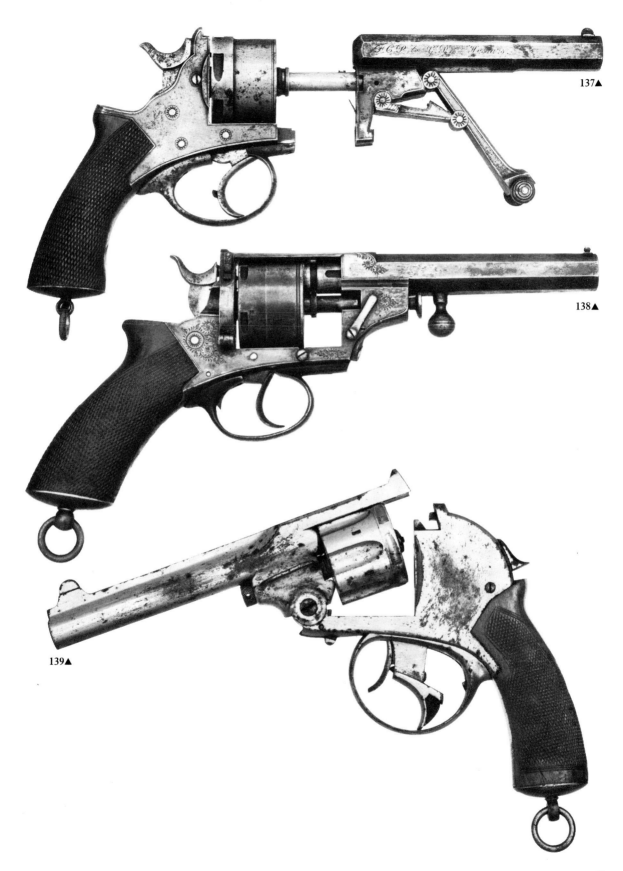

137▲

138▲

139▲

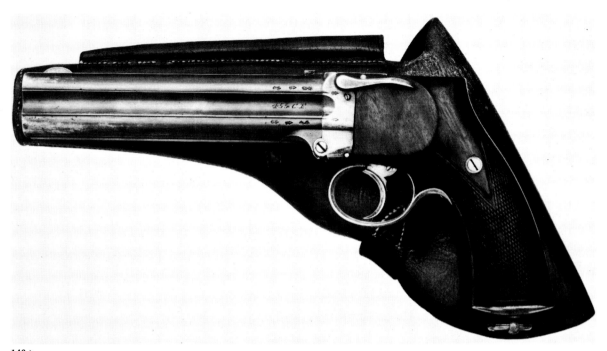

140▲

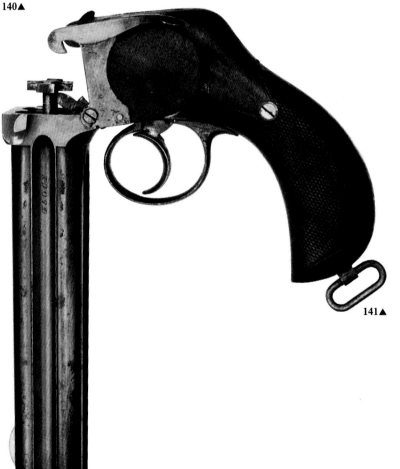

141▲

140–141. Although the revolver firing five to seven shots soon became the most popular pistol, gunmakers did not entirely forsake the multi-barrelled pistol, particularly when a pistol of large calibre and power was required. In 1881, the London gunmaker H. A. A. Thorn, trading as Charles Lancaster, patented a four-barrelled pistol, the barrels being hinged to the frame so that they dropped down in shotgun fashion for loading and extraction. A single, self-cocking trigger operated a revolving striker that fired the centre-fire cartridges in sequence. The pistols were made mainly in military calibres of .45in, .455in or .476in, and 'oval-bore' rifling allowed either shot or ball cartridges to be fired, lethal up to 40 yards. Two pistols are shown, the upper with its leather holster (**140**) and the lower open exposing its extractor (**141**). (XII.3523; XIII.193; XII.3522)

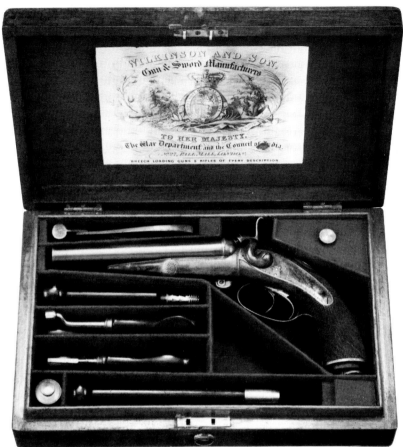

143▲

142▲

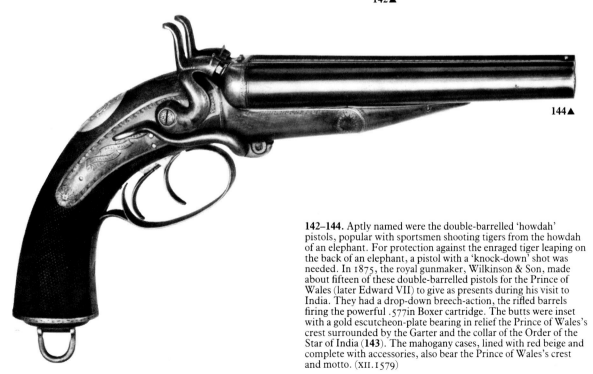

144▲

142–144. Aptly named were the double-barrelled 'howdah' pistols, popular with sportsmen shooting tigers from the howdah of an elephant. For protection against the enraged tiger leaping on the back of an elephant, a pistol with a 'knock-down' shot was needed. In 1875, the royal gunmaker, Wilkinson & Son, made about fifteen of these double-barrelled pistols for the Prince of Wales (later Edward VII) to give as presents during his visit to India. They had a drop-down breech-action, the rifled barrels firing the powerful .577in Boxer cartridge. The butts were inset with a gold escutcheon-plate bearing in relief the Prince of Wales's crest surrounded by the Garter and the collar of the Order of the Star of India (143). The mahogany cases, lined with red beige and complete with accessories, also bear the Prince of Wales's crest and motto. (XII.1579)

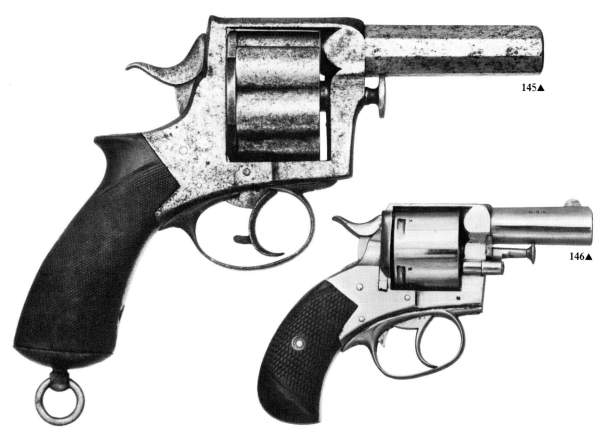

145, 146. With cartridges freely available, gunmakers like Webley & Scott of Birmingham produced revolvers for all occasions, from small dress pistols to large 'man-stoppers' like (**145**) which fires a large cartridge of Snider-rifle .577in calibre. Their popular 'British Bulldog' (**146**) was sold everywhere from 1878 to 1914, and widely copied by American and Belgian makers. This nickel-plated 5-shot model of .45in calibre has a typical 'parrot-beak' butt. (XII.5218; XII.3965)

147, 148. English gunmakers also copied American designs, particularly the rim-fire pocket models of Smith & Wesson, who held a manufacturing patent for guns with chambers bored through for cartridges. The upper revolver (**147**) is Smith & Wesson's No. 2 model 6-shot revolver of .32in calibre with tip-up barrel, sold by Walter Scott of Birmingham, about 1870. The lower (**148**) is a copy of Allen & Wheellock's 7-shot .22in calibre rim-fire revolver, engraved and proved in London. (XII.3946; XII.4824)

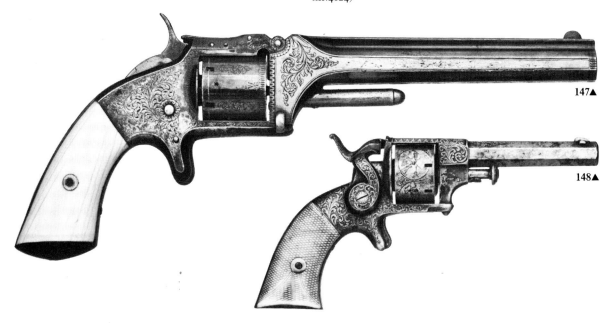

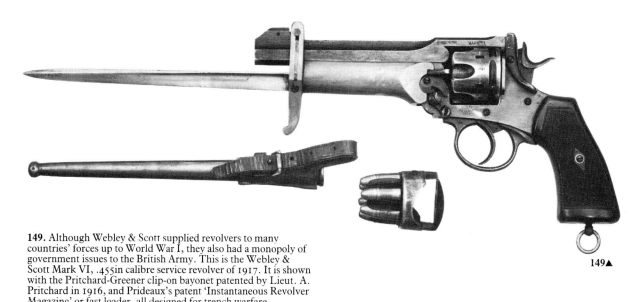

149. Although Webley & Scott supplied revolvers to many countries' forces up to World War I, they also had a monopoly of government issues to the British Army. This is the Webley & Scott Mark VI, .455in calibre service revolver of 1917. It is shown with the Pritchard-Greener clip-on bayonet patented by Lieut. A. Pritchard in 1916, and Prideaux's patent 'Instantaneous Revolver Magazine' or fast loader, all designed for trench warfare. (XII.3986)

149▲

150▲

150. Webley & Scott's Mark II service revolver was introduced in 1894. With the standard 4in barrel of .455/.476 calibre, this is a nickel-plated and engraved model and bears the firm's 'winged-bullet' trademark. The butt has been modified to carry the short spike-dagger patented by R. Gordon-Smith in 1897. It was intended for the same purpose as the 'skull-crusher' sometimes fitted to 18th-century pistol butts. (XII.3987)

151. The explosive power of a cartridge not only discharges the bullet but makes the pistol recoil. Gunmakers began to utilise this backward motion for automatic reloading. Col. G. V. Fosbery, V.C. obtained three patents for a recoil-operated revolver in 1895/6. In this Webley-Fosbery automatic revolver of 1901/2 the barrel and cylinder slide back and forth, cocking the hammer, while a stud on the frame acts in the zig-zag grooves cut in the cylinder to revolve it. (XII.3680)

152. The Mars automatic pistol was invented by Hugh Gabbett-Fairfax, who took out a number of patents between 1895 and 1900. It has a recoiling barrel and breech-block, the motion ejecting the fired case, reloading a new round from the box-magazine in the butt, and cocking the hammer ready to fire. Made in several models, that shown fired the high-velocity 8.5mm cartridge. Effective up to 100 yards, it was unpopular because of the vicious recoil. (XII.3677)

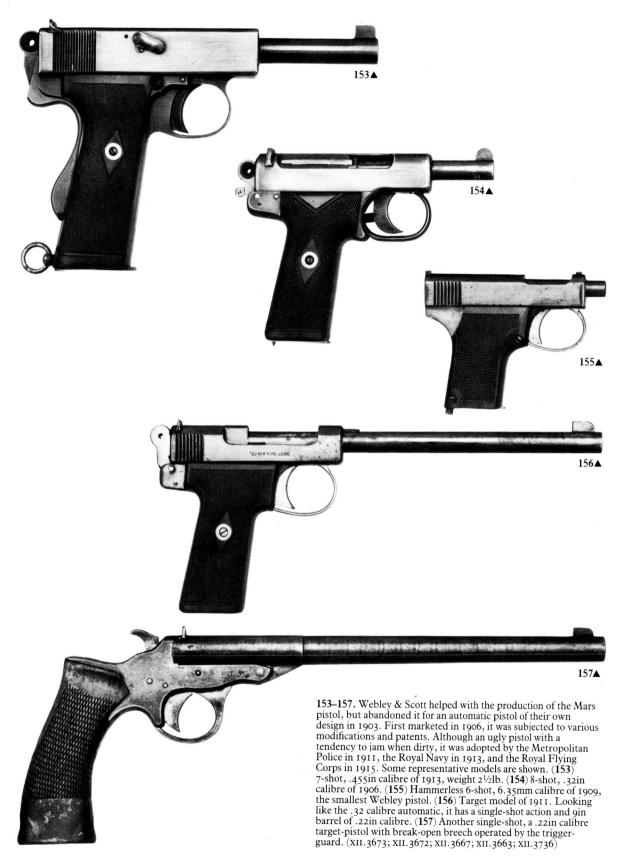

153–157. Webley & Scott helped with the production of the Mars pistol, but abandoned it for an automatic pistol of their own design in 1903. First marketed in 1906, it was subjected to various modifications and patents. Although an ugly pistol with a tendency to jam when dirty, it was adopted by the Metropolitan Police in 1911, the Royal Navy in 1913, and the Royal Flying Corps in 1915. Some representative models are shown. (**153**) 7-shot, .455in calibre of 1913, weight 2½lb. (**154**) 8-shot, .32in calibre of 1906. (**155**) Hammerless 6-shot, 6.35mm calibre of 1909, the smallest Webley pistol. (**156**) Target model of 1911. Looking like the .32 calibre automatic, it has a single-shot action and 9in barrel of .22in calibre. (**157**) Another single-shot, a .22in calibre target-pistol with break-open breech operated by the trigger-guard. (XII.3673; XII.3672; XII.3667; XII.3663; XII.3736)

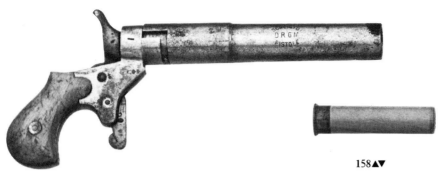

158. Dedles gas-pistol. This English version of the German 'Scheintot' ('apparent death') defensive arm was advertised in 1911 as rendering an adversary harmless without doing mortal or bodily injury. As the barrel had to be unclipped for loading the long 12mm calibre cartridge and then again to eject it with a rammer, it was advisable to make certain of one's shot, but a three-barrelled flat pistol for evening wear was available! (XII.5239)

158▲▼

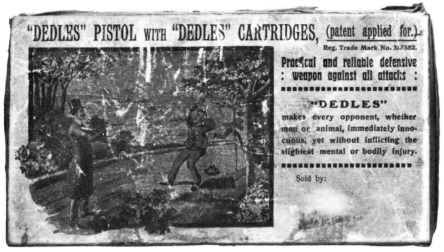

"DEDLES" PISTOL WITH "DEDLES" CARTRIDGES, (patent applied for.)

Reg. Trade Mark No. 315582.

Practical and reliable defensive
: weapon against all attacks :

▪▪▪▪▪▪▪▪▪▪▪▪▪▪▪▪▪▪▪▪▪▪▪▪▪▪▪

"DEDLES"

makes every opponent, whether man or animal, immediately innocuous, yet without inflicting the slightest mental or bodily injury.

▪▪▪▪▪▪▪▪▪▪▪▪▪▪▪▪▪▪▪▪▪▪▪▪▪▪▪

Sold by:

159▲

159. Flare or signal pistols had been in use as early as the 17th century, but the flare, when lit, remained attached to the pistol, its illumination often turning the holder into a target. In 1877, Lieut. E. W. Very of the U.S. Navy invented a pistol and cartridge which shot the flare high in the air before igniting it. This brass-barrelled Very-light pistol was made by Dyer & Robson, Greenwich, about 1885. (XII.5240)